DATE DUE

DOG DAYS

A Year in the
OSCAR MAYER WIENERMOBILE

Dave Ihlenfeld

STERLING
New York

STERLING
New York

An Imprint of Sterling Publishing
387 Park Avenue South
New York, NY 10016

© 2011 by Dave Ihlenfeld
Photographs © 2011 by Dave Ihlenfeld

ISBN 978-1-4027-9803-0 (paperback)
ISBN 978-1-4027-8966-3 (ebook)

Distributed in Canada by Sterling Publishing
c/o Canadian Manda Group, 165 Dufferin Street
Toronto, Ontario, Canada M6K 3H6
Distributed in the United Kingdom by GMC Distribution Services
Castle Place, 166 High Street, Lewes, East Sussex, England BN7 1XU
Distributed in Australia by Capricorn Link (Australia) Pty. Ltd.
P.O. Box 704, Windsor, NSW 2756, Australia

For information about custom editions, special sales, and premium and corporate purchases,
please contact Sterling Special Sales at 800-805-5489 or specialsales@sterlingpublishing.com.

Manufactured in the United States of America

2 4 6 8 10 9 7 5 3 1

www.sterlingpublishing.com

Author's Note

I tried to make this book as factually accurate as possible. But a few things are completely made up. First, the names (and some distinguishing features) of my fellow Hotdoggers have been changed to protect their privacy. They didn't sign up to be in a book, so I wanted to make sure they were shielded from what I'm sure will be an intense, undying interest in their real identities. I've also changed the names of friends and companions for the same reason. But, trust me, all these people really do exist.

I didn't bring a tape recorder on the road, so conversations are reconstructed through journal entries and to the best of my memory.

Special thanks to everyone who helped me relive my year on the road, especially the ever-patient Russ Whitacre and my Wienermobile colleagues. Twelve years later, I feel lucky to still have you all in my life.

Thanks to Candice Weiner (yes, her real name) for her outstanding research; to Tom Phillips, Phyllis Loverein, Bruce Kraig, Joe Kossack, and Rick Wood for consenting to be interviewed; to Jeff Schmidt for his salesmanship; to Russ Woody, David Goodman, and Steve Callaghan for their early encouragement; to Cherry and Win for their patient advice; to Leslie, Shaina, Jaydi, Ryan, and David for reading many terrible drafts; to Iris Blasi for her amazing editing; and to Audi for putting up with me.

Finally, a special thanks to Mom, Dad, and Matt for the continued support. To me, you're all top dogs.

Prologue

Journalism school doesn't teach what to do if you have to vomit during an interview.

The scene: An industrial bakery, October 1999. I'm here, my skin burning from the intense heat and my nose twitching from the overpowering scent of yeast, to interview a beat-down baker who looks as pale as the blob of dough that ferments next to him. I'm taping a story on bread—the many varieties, how it's made, and why people should eat it. Not exactly the hardest hitting news of the day. If I cared more about the subject, I probably wouldn't have stayed up drinking last night. That decision, one I've made many times during my college career, is now coming back to haunt me.

"I'm here every morning at four," the baker laments to the camera in a severe, scratchy monotone. "Then I work until nine at night—pounding dough, putting things in the oven, taking things out of the oven. Six days a week." The baker takes a long, thoughtful pause and then looks me straight in the eye. "Make sure you finish college, kid. Don't ever be a baker."

Then, as if the baker conjured it, the room gets very cold. The beads of sweat that were running down my forehead suddenly transform into tiny icicles.

"You see, the thing about bread is—" the baker continues, while my stomach churns and tosses.

I contemplate my options for a split second and then improvise a plan. "Excuse me," I say. "I think I left something in the car."

I'm out of my seat and race-walking toward the exit before the baker can say a word. I push open the door, lunge for my car, and put both hands on the hood to steady myself.

And that's when I start to vomit.

It's rare to experience a moment of clarity while throwing up breakfast, but I suddenly realize that I don't want to be a journalist. I don't want to drive to bakeries and interview bakers about baking. Really, I don't want to interview anyone about anything. I also don't want the stress, the long hours, and the shockingly low pay.

This is it—the sad end to my journalism career. The revelation is liberating.

The only bad thing is, I have no idea what I want to do instead.

November is not a good time to live in the sleepy college town of Columbia, Missouri. The October leaves, previously painted vibrant shades of red and orange, slowly brown before committing mass suicide. The University of Missouri Tigers football team similarly withers and dies. And the sky is either gray or black, no variations allowed.

I find myself in a strange position: For the first time, I have no direction in life, no next step. College ends in a few months, so I'm thinking it might be good to find those things. And quick.

I carry an overwhelming envy for the self-assured souls who already know their paths. Take my roommate Max, for example. He's never been what I would call self-reliant. Every weekend, Max returns home to St. Louis so his mom can do his laundry. And before he leaves campus for the two-hour drive home, Max calls his mom and tells her exactly what he wants for dinner. He gets steak, while I'm stuck with frozen fish sticks. The boy is pampered.

Yet, somehow Max has his future figured out. He'll get a master's in accounting, move back to St. Louis, and find a job at some esteemed firm with cool initials. Life will be good to Max. And I'll continue to eat fish sticks.

Another fraternity brother, Spencer, will go to work at his dad's electrical company, marry his high school sweetheart, and buy a boat. The only difficult life decision Spencer has to make will be if he wants an inboard or outboard motor.

Perhaps part of the problem is my family. My parents are sweet, loving folks, but they've always had a plan for the future. My father, a self-made man from Milwaukee, started working for IBM right out of college and stayed with them for more than thirty years. He married, moved to the suburbs, and had two kids.

My mother attended an all-women's college in Missouri, spent a few years as a gym teacher, and then married my father. I came along two years later. I'm not sure if she had grander ambitions than being a doting mother, but if she did, we certainly never suffered from resentment.

Then there's my younger brother. We're two years apart and had a playfully antagonistic relationship growing up. We delighted in competing with one another, and I delighted in usually winning. I also loved playing mind games with him. Before important swim meets I would hide notes in my brother's gym bag that said, "Don't embarrass the Ihlenfeld name."

Our most intense rivalry took place in the basement, on a wrestling mat made of leftover shag carpeting. There we started the CWA—the Child Wrestling Alliance. For years we fought over the federation's most prestigious prize—a title belt made of poster board and gold glitter. I first won that belt when I was ten, and I'm proud to say that I'm still champion.

Unable to beat me in meaningless contests, my brother decided to focus on actual accomplishments. He recently started his sophomore year at the Air Force Academy. Not only is he getting paid to go to school, but he's also selflessly serving his country. I find myself awkwardly looking up to the kid who once looked up to me. And *I'm* the one with the championship belt!

With graduation stalking me like a hungry puma, my new plan is to interview for anything. Farm equipment sales, Jacuzzi installation, salad bar inspector—bring it on! People get jobs every day; surely there's one for me.

My first interview is with a large computer firm. Because of my dad's IBM pedigree, I hope to be genetically inclined for the field. And while I've never been particularly interested in computers, I dutifully put on my only suit (the one with the sleeves that stop just below the elbows) and trudge to the interview.

"Always carry a folder," my father once told me. "It gives you something to hold on to." Remembering his advice, I defensively clutch a gray binder as I meet with Tom, a boyish-looking recruiter who moves around with the crazed, erratic energy of a coked-up hummingbird. This guy obviously loves his work. We sit down and I hand Tom a freshly printed resume. Slowly his right eyebrow begins to rise.

"So you're a broadcast journalism major?" he asks.

I feel this may be a trick question, but decide to answer honestly. "Yes."

"And you're interested in computer sales?" he says in a slightly disbelieving tone.

I try to combat his doubt with fake enthusiasm. "I'm *very* interested. My father sold computers for thirty years and loved it. He bought a house and put two kids through college with that job. I think I could be just as successful."

Tom nods his head.

He's buying it, I tell myself. Just a few more lies and I can go home.

Now convinced of my sincerity, Tom starts getting excited and decides to make this an actual interview. "What's your greatest weakness?"

Ahhh...my favorite question. The trick is making a weakness sound like a strength. "I'm a perfectionist," I respond. "I like to do things right and I get frustrated if people don't share my commitment to excellence."

Tom's face lights up. "That's our motto!" He pulls out a white T-shirt from under the table and holds it up like some prized trout. COMMITMENT TO EXCELLENCE is printed on the back. It really is their motto.

"Here, you can keep this!" he says. "Wow...that's great you knew our motto." Tom stands up and shakes my hand. "We'll be in touch. Definitely."

But Tom never calls. To spite him, I end up using the T-shirt as a dishrag.

I go on a few more interviews. Not because I want to, but because I'm supposed to. There's the 11 p.m. to 6 a.m. editing shift at a small Kansas City TV station, a job passing out credit card applications on campus, and the chance to proofread magazine articles. I'm somewhat qualified for all of them, but don't get any. Never underestimate the power of a liberal arts education.

I'm not the only one who's pessimistic about my future. I showed my resume to my highly regarded political science professor in the hope that he could point me toward a career path. His written response was anything but encouraging: "I have looked over your resume. What I see is a fellow who got trapped by a j-school that is more like a vo-tech program. Given your considerable horsepower, a strong liberal arts and strong science major would have been better. Needless to say, I have seen this several times before at Missouri. Ugh."

"Ugh" is never something you want to see written on your resume.

After that cheery assessment, I'm just about ready to give up and resign myself to a life of bland, meaningless productivity. It worked for Sting. But then my job search took an unexpected turn.

Signs began appearing around the journalism school trumpeting a chance to "Travel the Hot Dog Highways." What I first thought to be some perverted joke turned out to be an announcement that the Oscar Mayer Wienermobile would soon be recruiting on campus.

The Wienermobile recruits? For what? Pit crews? Wiener waxers?

Like any red-blooded American, I knew what the Wienermobile is. But I'd never seen it in person. Nor had I had a desire to see it. I realized it was big and shaped like a hot dog, but I didn't quite understand the allure of wacky promotional vehicles.

And yet, something about the sign intrigued me. What are the "Hot Dog Highways," where did they go, and, most importantly, how much did they pay? Curious, and with absolutely no better options, I signed up for an interview. Desperate men do dumb things.

CHAPTER 1

So you grew up in Naperville," says the man behind the desk in a deep, Midwestern baritone.

His name is Russ Whitacre and he's the manager of the Wienermobile program. Russ is a large, somewhat round man who looks like a cross between a bear and the Pillsbury Doughboy. He has neat brown hair, carefully parted to the side, and wears a short-sleeve polo shirt despite the frost.

"Yes, I was born in Milwaukee and moved to Naperville when I was two," I respond politely.

The setting of my Wienermobile interview is a small, barren office in a dark corner of a journalism classroom building that seems better fit for an interrogation than an interview. Russ looks like he's been crowbarred into the tiny space.

"Naperville, huh?" Russ responds. "So you know the Jewel store on Washington and Ogden?"

"Uh . . . yeah," I reply slowly, surprised by the intimate knowledge of my hometown geography. "I lived right down the street from there."

Now *I* have a few questions. Like, how does this man know about the Jewel grocery store on Washington and Ogden? Does he have some sick obsession with suburban strip malls?

"Nice place, Naperville," says Russ, as if lost in a fond memory. His eyes eventually return to my resume. "So you're a broadcast journalism major?"

Not *that* question again.

"Yes . . . I am," I reply, then stop. I can't think of more to say on the subject. Russ shows some mercy and moves on to the next bullet point.

"Says here you did an internship in Los Angeles last summer. What inspired that?"

I relate the charming story of my time in Los Angeles. I didn't have a great reason for going beyond wanting to see the city and gain some exposure to the entertainment industry. Maybe there was a fleeting thought of being discovered, but that faded after an aspiring starlet took one look at my flannel plaid shirt (buttoned to the very top) and asked if I had just fallen off a truck. I was crushed.

I lived with five roommates, all strangers from Missouri, in an apartment complex that is more known for housing child actors than college students. Since our cramped unit had a total of four beds, I had to sleep on a cot hastily stolen from the hall. Once again, I was crushed.

It was a summer of strange experiences that would be hard to embellish. To celebrate my first night in town, my roommates took me to a bar called Mickey's in West Hollywood. Having never been to Mickey's (or West Hollywood), I had no idea what to expect. The picture became a bit clearer when the first thing I saw upon entering was a topless man in cutoff jean shorts and a tool belt dancing on a cube. Turns out that Mickey's is a gay bar. It was the first time I'd been in a bar where the line for the men's room was longer than the line for the women's.

If there's one word to describe my summer in Los Angeles it's "peculiar." Four of my five roommates turned out to be gay. Peculiar. I had three jobs: organizing file boxes in a law office, interning at a film development company, and teaching swim lessons to a rich thirteen-year-old in her Beverly Hills backyard. Peculiar. And our upstairs neighbors were hip-hop star Usher, and his mom. Peculiar.

I breathlessly go on about my summer travails and, for the first time, Russ seems somewhat impressed. "We like it when people show some independence," he says.

I leave the interview still having no idea what driving the Wiener-mobile is all about. But I do know it's an option. And I have precious few of those right now.

Later, I call my parents and tell them about the interview. Like me, they aren't quite sure what to make of the Wienermobile.

"So they pay you to drive around in a hot dog?" asks my mom.

"Yes."

"And where do you live? In the hot dog?" she inquires.

"No, you stay in hotels."

"And how long do you do this for?"

"One year."

"And you just drive around?"

"Yes."

"In a hot dog?"

"Yes," I say with a sigh. This conversation is going about as well as expected.

"How much does it pay?"

"$21,000."

"That's it?"

"That's it. But they do pay for food and lodging."

"What do you do after it ends?"

"Find something else, I guess."

"And this is really a job?"

"Yes, Mom, it's really a job."

That last one was a lie. I'm not sure if it's really a job.

CHAPTER 2

Oscar Mayer headquarters smells like bacon. When that Madison wind blows just right, a warm, smoky aroma is your greeting to cold cut country. It's 6:30 in the morning and I'm on a hotel shuttle that's driving toward destiny. Or disappointment.

A few weeks ago, Russ called to say that I was one of sixty people the company wanted to fly to Madison, Wisconsin, for second-round interviews. The finalists have been divided into a number of groups, so, for the next day and a half, I only have to worry about being better than ten other people. Last night, we all bonded over beer and mozzarella sticks at the hotel bar. Today, we're at war.

Sitting next to me in the back of this cramped van is Jane, a short, serious girl who seems deadly focused on driving the Wienermobile. She tightly grips a large black notebook (a move she stole from my father) and stares out at the gray landscape. Even with such rigid posture, Jane is the picture of cute; her brown hair done in a discreet bob that perfectly frames her face.

"Smells like bacon," I say in an attempt at finding common ground.

Jane turns her head ever so slightly. "You'll get used to it."

Already, I'm a bit worried by the amount of effort some of these

4

prospects put into applying. One girl brought along a hot dog-shaped diorama. Another made a video of herself tap dancing to the Oscar Mayer jingle. A guy sent his resume wrapped around a pack of hot dogs. That's certainly one way to get attention.

"What did you do to make it here?" someone asked me last night.

"I, uh, interviewed on campus," I said.

"That was it?"

"Yeah, that was it."

The group was shocked.

Our ragtag crew of wannabe Hotdoggers debarks the shuttle and enters the relatively modest Oscar Mayer headquarters. A bored receptionist points us toward the even more modest Conference Room B, which resembles a well-lit holding pen. Russ is planted in the front of the room, silently waiting. Somehow he seems bigger than I remember.

Russ's opening speech is little more than "good morning" and "welcome to Madison." There's no sense wasting time on unnecessary pleasantries, especially since a majority of us will never be back here.

The next six hours are interview after long, boring interview. I meet Joy, the department's scheduling guru and second in command. She must be in her early fifties, but she moves and talks much faster than I. She has short auburn hair and wears makeup carefully chosen to match her colorful outfit. She may be a third the size of Russ, but her personality is just as big.

"Do you know how to balance a checkbook?" Joy asks.

"Sure. I do it every month."

"That's a relief. You wouldn't believe how many Hotdoggers can't add or subtract."

Wait . . . this job requires math? No one mentioned anything about math.

"Have you ever been in an accident?"

"I got pulled over for speeding once," I say.

"When was that?"

"Six years ago maybe."

"But no accidents?"

"Nope."

"That's good. Everyone's got speeding tickets."

My next interview is with Tommy, the shaggy, free-spirited Wienermobile advisor. His job is to serve as a liaison between the Hot-doggers on the road and the managers in the office. Tommy takes a cursory glance at my resume and then pushes it aside. We spend the next thirty minutes talking about our favorite Monty Python routines.

"Wow, that didn't hurt much," I say when our time is up.

"Well, if I have to ask questions based on your resume, you're probably not going to get the job."

The next stop is Cyndi, head of PR for Oscar Mayer. This woman is serious. She doesn't even giggle when saying "wiener."

As soon as I sit down, Cyndi makes it clear that this is more cross-examination than interview. She studies my resume for a long time then looks up and locks her tiny eyes on mine. "How would you handle some-one protesting the Wienermobile, Mr. Ill-len-field?"

"Why would anyone protest the Wienermobile?" I ask.

"Various reasons," responds Cyndi. "How would you handle such a situation?"

I venture a wild guess. "By talking to them?"

Cyndi cocks an eyebrow. "And what if you couldn't talk to them?"

"I, um, would call the office?"

Cyndi sighs before scribbling something down on her notepad.

The interview wheel next stops with Dan. I never find out his exact job title, but I'm assuming it involves A/V since his musty office is littered with bulky VCRs, dusty TVs, and some orphan circuit boards.

Dan sits me on a tall stool and turns a video camera toward me. "All right, let me just get set up here. Just a few adjustments . . . Don't worry, this won't hurt a bit."

I fight back the broadcast journalism flashbacks and try to appear relaxed and comfortable. It's not easy when the only part of Dan not blocked by the camera is his wide, carp-like mouth. I hope he didn't lure me in here for murder. Or to help him try on pants.

The camera's red light blinks on and Dan points at me. "Dave, what is your most embarrassing moment?"

Suddenly I feel very icky. Fortunately, I've already been asked this question twice today and can answer without thinking. "I was swimming in this big, championship meet and halfway through the race my suit starting falling off. So I had to paddle with one hand and hold my suit up with the other."

Dan laughs, enjoying my embarrassment. After a few more videotaped questions, he gets a chance to embarrass me more. "Okay, we're almost wrapped up here. We just need to get you on tape singing the 'I Wish I Were' jingle."

"What? Really?"

"Yup. Just belt it out."

"I'm not a very good singer."

"That's okay."

The jingle that Jim's referring to was written by Richard Trentlage, a Chicago ad man, in 1963. At the time, J. Walter Thompson was running a contest to find a new Oscar Mayer jingle and Trentlage got a call asking if he was going to enter. Unfortunately, the deadline was the next morning. So, according to the *Oxford Encyclopedia of Food and Drink in America*, Trentlage quickly wrote the tune and then recorded it at home with his young son and daughter doing the vocals. Oscar G. Mayer loved the jingle and insisted that Trentlage's kids stay on record as the singers. The jingle debuted on the radio and later became a television ad. Jerry Ringlien, who worked in the Oscar Mayer advertising department at the time, described the "Wish I Were" campaign as "the commercial that took Oscar Mayer to national distribution." It's now the longest-running jingle in America.

Eleven years later, in 1974, Ringlien created a jingle that's almost as famous: "My bologna has a first name . . ."

"Anytime you're ready," says Dan, snapping me back to the cruel fact that I'm actually going to have to sing on camera. I clear my throat, put on my bravest face, and give a terribly off-key rendition of Trentlage's tune.

"Oh I wish I were an Oscar Mayer wiener . . ."

"Great! Just great," says Dan.

I now have a new most embarrassing moment.

After that humiliation, I'm almost relieved to see that my next interview is with Russ. I have a seat in his quaint, windowless office and get ready to be grilled. Since we already covered my neighborhood groceries in the first round, Russ moves on to the harder questions. "So, David, why do you want to be a Hotdogger?"

Uh-oh.

It's the question I've been most dreading, far more than "What's your most embarrassing moment?" or "When is that acne going to clear up?" I flew to Madison and willingly subjected myself to six hours of interviews; doesn't that speak to my passion for the position? But Russ, wise old Russ, has called my bluff.

There are two answers to the question, the truthful one I tell myself and the business reply I tell Russ. Let me give the internal answer first.

I don't want to be a Hotdogger. In fact, I'm still not even sure what a Hotdogger does. Trust me, this is not where I expected to be toward the end of my college days. I pictured myriad job offers and a clear idea of which one to take. I expected happiness, success, and the envy of all my classmates. Hell, I thought I'd at least have a girlfriend. So if I'm being completely honest, the reason I'm applying to be a Hotdogger is because it's a job. With pay.

Now, the answer I actually give: "I want to be a Hotdogger because it's the adventure of a lifetime. I mean, how often do you get paid to travel the country while talking about hot dogs? I just think it would be an amazing opportunity to learn and grow and meet all sorts of people and be part of such a unique opportunity."

Russ stares blankly at me for a second. He knows I'm lying. But then, just as I'm about to bolt for the door, Russ nods. "Yes, it is quite an opportunity," he says quietly.

I return to Columbia none the wiser, none the happier, and none the clearer. If not an Oscar Mayer Wiener, what is it I truly want to be?

One day I return home from class, excited about watching two full hours of *Beverly Hills 90210*, and see a blinking red light on the answering machine. I press PLAY.

"Hello, David!" says a voice that leaps out of the machine. "This is Russ Whitacre from the Oscar Mayer Wienermobile program. Give us a call at your earliest convenience."

I know instantly—they want to offer me the job. Sure, Russ could be calling to let me down easy, but there's something in his voice, some hint of previously hidden happiness, that says they like me . . . they really like me.

That's when panic sets in. Do I really want to spend a year trapped inside a hot dog?

Incapable of making such a hefty life decision on my own, I quickly call my parents. They'll tell me what to do.

"Mom, Dad . . . I think Oscar Mayer wants to offer me the Wiener-mobile job."

There's a beat of silence on the other end. I can sympathize with my parents' dilemma. They have two children on completely opposite ends of the son spectrum. One is at the Air Force Academy, learning how to pilot fighter jets, and the other is thinking about driving a sausage car. Talk about different ways of serving your country.

"That's great!" says Mom.

"Wow. Congratulations!" says Dad.

I can't believe my parents are excited about this. I'm not even excited about this. "I don't know. I'm not sure if I should take it."

My mom gasps. "David! Why wouldn't you take it?"

"Well, it's a year commitment. And I'm not sure where you can go after that."

"Oh sweetie, you have to take it," says Mom immediately. "You would regret passing up this opportunity. Just think of all the people you'd get to meet and the places you'd get to go. It would be neat."

"Not many people get to do something like this," agrees Dad.

My parents have always enjoyed road trips. When my brother and I were young, they drove us from Chicago to Washington, DC, in our Oldsmobile station wagon. The only thing I remember about the trek is being so hot that I had to keep peeling my sticky skin off the leather seats.

The trips were long, but my parents stressed the importance of keeping the family together. That meant always taking Buffy, our hyperactive golden retriever, who hated nothing more than being caged in the back of a station wagon. She would buck and scratch and howl for the entire trip, drowning out all attempts at family bonding up front. But my parents persevered. Once they decided to calm Buffy with a tranquilizer. Minutes later, Buffy's eyes were glazed over and she was whimpering like a far-away smoke alarm. Two hours in, poor Buffy was slumped against the back window. To my traumatized brother and me, it looked like our parents had just killed the family dog.

"Don't worry," reassured my dad. "She's not dead. She's just very, very tired."

Despite my parents' obvious appreciation for adventure, I'm shocked by their enthusiastic reaction to my news. "You really think I should do this?" I ask.

"David, you'll be a success at whatever you choose to do," says Dad. "So if it's driving the Wienermobile for a year, go for it. You're young, you can still get away with things like that." He pauses for a moment. "Of course, you don't want to be forty and still fooling around."

"Well, thanks," I say. "I'll think about it."

"Good luck, David," says Dad. "You'll do the right thing."

"We're very proud of you," says Mom.

Damn those people, always showing me love and support.

I spend a few minutes pacing the hall. The choice comes down to choices. It's the Wienermobile versus nothing, Hotdogger versus unemployed loser. Not too difficult a decision when put in such stark terms. I call Russ and accept the job. If I must have a next chapter in my life, it might as well be an interesting one.

CHAPTER 3

O scar Ferdinand Mayer was born in Kaesingen, Wuerttemburg, a small town near the Bavarian border, on March 29, 1859. Historically, the men in his family were ministers and forest-ers, although Mayer's immediate family ran a small grocery business in Nuremberg. That shop failed in the early 1870s, and, in 1873, fourteen-year-old Mayer emigrated to the United States with his cousin John M. Schroll, becoming a butcher boy at George Weber's meat market in Detroit. Three years later, the Schrolls left for Chicago and brought young Oscar with them.

It was in Chicago that Oscar Mayer's meat-making career really took off. He apprenticed in the stockyards of Armour & Co. and worked at Kohlhammer's meat market on Chicago's near north side. Eager to start his own business, Oscar wrote home and convinced his sausage-making brother Gottfried to leave Nuremberg and join him in America.

In 1883, the Mayer brothers leased the failing Kolling Meat Market on Chicago's north side and went into business for themselves. "The early days weren't easy," said Mayer's grandson, Oscar G. Mayer Jr. "First day sales were $59, not really too bad when you recall that pork cuts sold at eight to twelve cents a pound then."

Brother Max soon ventured to America and took over the shop's bookkeeping. *Over time, Oscar Mayer and his brothers built a profitable store that catered to the mostly German neighborhood. In 1888, the Kollings saw a chance to capitalize on the store's success and refused to renew the Mayers' lease. Undaunted, the Mayer brothers borrowed $10,000 and bought their own place a few blocks away. The two-story building had a shop on the first floor and living quarters on the second.*

A 1968 Time *magazine article describes the early days of the Mayers' business. "The Bavarian Mayer brothers worked hard stuffing sausages. Oscar's wife Louise helped, and their son Oscar G. stood on a butter tub behind the counter to take orders. Weisswurst, Bockwurst, Leberwurst were packed into wicker baskets and piled on horse-drawn wagons to make the rounds. They sold well enough to send Oscar G. to Harvard." According to Oscar G. Jr., Gottfried kept the sausage and spice recipes in a "well-guarded little black book."*

The Mayers' shop was a great success and customers were often waiting in lines that stretched out the door. While most meat markets delivered large orders on foot, the Mayers packed theirs into wicker baskets and used horse-drawn wagons to reach Chicago and suburban customers. At the turn of the century "there were 43 employees, including, among others, five wagon salesmen, one pig-head-and-feet cleaner and cooker, and two stablemen to take care of the delivery horses."

In 1911, company assets totaled $300,000. By 1918, sales at Oscar Mayer would reach $11 million.

CHAPTER 4

t's nearing the end of senior year. When people have asked what I'm doing after graduation, I usually just tell them, "I don't know." It's easier than saying, "I'm going to be a Hotdogger."

But now the job is very real. I've even started getting mail from Oscar Mayer:

Congratulations on becoming part of Hotdoggers XII. We look forward to seeing you in Madison on June 8 for Hot Dog High. Please contact Tommy in the Wienermobile Department to arrange travel to Madison. Your team assignment is below.

California Team:
David (University of Missouri)
Sofia (University of Florida)
Ali (University of Missouri)
Brad (University of Texas)

The letter is my first concrete glimpse of the year ahead and I study it like some mad forensic scientist. The only thing I can reliably discern is that our team will have four people: two guys and two girls. That seems pretty concrete. Let's hope at least one of the girls is smoking hot.

I'm surprised to see a fellow Missouri student on the list. How did this person elude me through two rounds of interviews?

It turns out that Ali lives a few houses down from me. Strange that two people so involved with processed meat have never met before. To rectify this before Hot Dog High, we arrange to have lunch at a nearby deli.

"How will I find you?" I ask over the phone.

"Just look for the blonde hair," she responds.

Sure enough, I spot the hair before I've even entered the restaurant. Her long, curly locks are a vivid yellow, the kind of yellow that would make a dandelion jealous. I enter and tentatively approach my new partner.

"Hi, I'm Dave."

"I'm Ali."

Before I can offer my hand, Ali envelops me in a tight hug. I'm not used to so much affection from a total stranger and I awkwardly respond with some soft pats on her back. We pick a table in the back and she's talking before I can even sit down.

"Do you know Derrick Heinz?" she asks.

"No."

"Debbie Brantley?"

"No."

"They're both advertising majors. They got hired, too."

"Wow, four Missouri students. I wonder—"

"Do you know Mike Simpson?"

"No. Is he—"

"He's a former Hotdogger. He's the one who actually told me about the job." I'm beginning to realize that Ali is a lot more popular than I.

"So you actually knew this job existed?" I ask.

"Oh yeah," she says, cocking me a strange look. "Didn't you?"

"No, I just found out about it because they put some posters up around the J-school."

"Oh."

"To be honest, I wasn't even sure I wanted the job."

Ali looks like I just stole her puppy. "Really? I wanted it."

I decide I have to do some backtracking and put on a happy face. "Oh yeah, now I'm looking forward to it. Can't wait."

Conversation with Ali is easy, mostly because she does 95 percent of the talking. Besides the hair, Ali has an immense smile that perfectly matches her expansive, green eyes. Her skin is fair, her face oval-shaped and uniquely expressive. Almost every word gets its own muscle movement. Ali radiates a sort of happy energy that compels you to like her. It's easy to see why she was hired.

It's just too bad she's giving me a sisterly vibe. I don't have a sister, but I'm pretty sure you can't make out with them.

We soon finish our lunch and say good-bye. "See you on the road!" she says. "It's going to be great!"

This time, I'm ready for the hug. Hot Dog High, here we come.

Please let that be her. Please let that be her.

I'm standing at Gate 7 of the Dane Country Regional Airport in Madison, Wisconsin, as strangers file by. This solitary terminal, so calm and serene on my last visit, is now bustling with unprecedented energy. The Hotdoggers have begun to arrive.

My new teammates meet and greet and hug and handshake in the background, a whirlwind of introductory bliss that's hard to ignore. But I ignore it. I can't be bothered with making new friends yet because I'm on a mission to meet exactly one person: my partner Sofia.

Through the crowd of disembarking passengers, I spot Ali walking down the jetway with a striking stranger.

Please let that be her. Please let that be her.

The woman isn't "cute" or "attractive"—she's gorgeous. Tall with a tan complexion, long brown hair bouncing happily around her angular face, shimmering eyes, and confident cheekbones. Such exotic features look completely out of place in the white-bread Dane County Regional Airport.

My mind races at the prospect that this woman, this heavenly vision, might be my teammate.

Please let that be her. Please let that be her.

"There's Dave!" says Ali when she spies me doing a nervous jig by the gate. She drops her bags and gives me a hug. It's difficult to commit while I'm sneaking peeks at her brown-eyed traveling companion.

Ali breaks the embrace and gestures to her new sidekick. "This is Sofia. We met on the plane."

Praise be ... it is her!

"Hi, I'm Dave Ihlenfeld," I say while rigidly offering my right hand.

Sofia looks at it quizzically for a moment, as if I'm offering her a piece of toast. "Hi, I'm Sofia," she says as she grips my hand and gives it a firm, almost sarcastic shake. "Nice to meet you, Dave Ihlenfeld."

"Nice to, uh, meet you too. I, um—"

But before I can ask about her trip or propose marriage, Sofia is quickly engulfed by the group and forced to endure a gauntlet of hugs. I step back and give thanks for my blessed luck. For the next few months, I'll be sitting shotgun next to a super-hot chick. This could be the greatest career move ever.

CHAPTER 5

Yes, Virginia, there is a Hot Dog High.

When the Wienermobile returned in 1988 (after being off the road since 1977), the sales and marketing people were eager to harness its awesome promotional powers and pushed to get the vehicles on the road as soon as possible. But the embryonic Wienermobile department realized that it might be a good idea to take a few days and actually train these pioneering Hotdoggers. And so Hot Dog High was born.

In the beginning, Hot Dog High lasted only four and a half days. "It was pretty much come in, sit down in a classroom, here are some things to help the company, here's what your job's going to be, here's how to fill out an expense report, and here are the keys," remembers Russ. Now, Hot Dog High is a two-week boot camp, where naïve college graduates are molded into courteous, media-savvy, pun-wielding Hotdoggers. The program is long, intensive, and mentally challenging. It even claimed a New Mexico State grad who got so intimidated by the other Hotdoggers that he asked to be sent home after two days.

Hotdoggers XII is a gang of thirteen fresh-faced college grads. The complete roster includes me, Jane (my interview shuttle partner), Ali, Luke, Ben, Derrick, Candace, Leah, Debbie, Jamila, Shawna, Melissa, and, of course, Sofia. Our California teammate Brad and seven other Hotdoggers from group XI are currently on the road and will be joining us in a week.

This merry band has been together for only a few hours, but already everyone acts like old friends. It's amazing how quickly strangers can bond over a shared job and some meat-related puns. And, of course, generous amounts of alcohol don't hurt.

We're all gathered for a welcome dinner at one of Madison's finest "grill your own meat" restaurants. Russ is in fine spirits. "David! Glad you could join us!" he roars when I enter the dining room. Eagerly, I make the rounds to get better acquainted with some of these strange new people.

There's Melissa, a University of Colorado graduate with a sweet, almost angelic face that masks a loud and deeply sarcastic personality. Melissa marches right over to me. "From now on, I'm Mustard Melissa. Let's go have a drink." Already she's one of my favorites.

Leah also went to Colorado. She's a quiet, unassuming girl who spends most of the evening nervously clutching a drink and standing in view of the exit. I cautiously approach, careful not to make any sudden movements, and ask how she's doing. "I'm terrified," she confesses. "This is the most Type A personalities I've ever been with in my life."

Derrick, a rather large black man who would be intimidating if he weren't so friendly, is a fellow Missouri Tiger. Derrick bravely turned down a prestigious internship with music company EMI even though Oscar Mayer hadn't offered him a position yet. Somehow Derrick just knew that being a Hotdogger was the only job he wanted, Mizzou has the largest contingent of Hotdoggers in our class. There's me, Derrick, Ali, and Debbie, an advertising major with a surprisingly firm handshake. Like Derrick, Debbie only had eyes for the Wienermobile. "I didn't send my resume to anyone. I didn't have any other jobs, and it was all eggs in one basket," she tells me when we meet.

"Why did you want to do it so bad?"

"I don't know. It sounded cool. I hadn't really researched it much. It's not like I was six and wanted to do this my whole life. But I was sold on it."

Luke, a lanky, clean-cut graduate of William and Mary, sent in a crazy, pun-filled cover letter in the Wienermobile colors. "I took the job because I wanted to see the country. I've never been outside of the East Coast. Actually, I'd only been on a plane once before my interview here."

"Did you tell that to Russ?"

"No," he says with a laugh. "I don't think I brought that up."

While I like my fellow employees immediately, Sofia is really the only one I love. Or, to be more accurate, the only one I intend to fall in love with. Emboldened after a few beers, I strategically pick a seat next to her at the long banquet hall.

"So, you liking Hot Dog High?"

"Yeah, it's like summer camp," she says in a warm, low octave that makes me happy to be alive.

"How'd you end up here?"

"It was one of those random things," she says with a laugh. "The Wienermobile didn't make it to our school to recruit. Then I read that the Wienermobile was coming into town for a singing competition and I decided to enter my little brother. So we went and I realized how awesome the Wienermobile was. I started talking to one of the Hotdoggers and she said it was the best job ever. I took her card and figured if I didn't know what I wanted to do by the time I graduated, I would apply."

"That's what happened to me. Well, the not knowing what to do part."

"Cool."

Before I can make any more progress, Russ stands up at the head table and taps his glass to quiet everyone down. It takes quite a few clinks to calm this crowd, but eventually all eyes are on Russ.

"Welcome to Hot Dog High," he says. "You were hired because you demonstrated independence and initiative." Russ gestures across the room. "Ben spent a month walking across Spain. Ali scooped lemon ice at Walt Disney World for a summer. David drove out to Los Angeles and interned at a film production company." So that's why I was hired! My restless spirit must have made up for my complete lack of enthusiasm.

"You all went off the block and didn't go home every weekend," Russ continues. "You all took risks. That's what we want. We want people who can go to Puck City, Oklahoma, and be curious about what's there."

Russ then moves on to what will be expected of us in the coming year. "There are three P's involved with being a Hotdogger: patience, performance, and people. Patience, as in don't snap at the customers. Performance, as in flawlessly execute all events. And people, as in talk to them.

"Soak in all you can, keep your eyes open, seek out all opportunities, and be flexible. You're part of a team now, and while we don't expect you to be best friends, we do expect mutual respect, working together, and doing the job." After a beat, Russ continues. "Okay, everyone please stand up."

As the crowd rises, Russ unfurls a wrinkled piece of paper from his jacket pocket. "The Hotdogger Oath. Please repeat after me," he announces in a most serious voice. "As an official Hotdogger of the celebrated Oscar Mayer Wienermobile, I salami swear to uphold the dogma set forth here, and I promise to: Encourage wiener lovers nationwide to relish the delicacy, ketchup on the great taste of hot dogs, and give in to the craving once it's mustard. Be frank and, furthermore, to be upstanding in a line for hot dogs at ballparks, barbecues, buffets, and other bashes. Journey into the streets, dachs, und ports of my community, wish well to all comers, plump and lean—and leave them with a wiener to roast about. As once I wished I were, now I am—an Oscar Mayer Wienermobile Hotdogger."

We dutifully repeat each sentence and let out a loud cheer at the end. Our group now has an identity. We're Hotdoggers.

Geez, that's such a dumb name.

CHAPTER 6

Nothing can possibly be that orange. That's my first impression of the Wienermobile—an impossibly large, improbably colored vehicle.

Like a proud papa, Russ is giving the new hires a tour of the machines he helped design and push through production. And it's about time. We're already a few days into Hot Dog High and so far it's been nothing but expense reports, repair forms, benefit packages, hearing tests, and current events quizzes. Why current events quizzes? Because, according to Russ, "It's important to know what's going on."

There's also the added bonus of getting up at 6:30 every morning and having meetings from eight to five. This is more corporate boot camp than high school. "I'm surprised it's so serious," Jamila jokes during training. "You hear 'Hot Dog High' and expect clown school." I can't help but agree.

So far there have only been a few Hot Dog High highlights. One was the mention of a possible tour of U.S. military bases in Europe. If it happens, the company would pick two people to pilot the Wienermobile around the continent, most expenses paid.

"I'll do it! I'll do it!" I offered, my mind swimming with the possibility of a romantic getaway with Sofia. I could propose under the Eiffel Tower!

"We'll see, David," chastised Russ. "Please sit back down."

We also received our schedules. Team California starts, appropriately enough, in California. We spend a few months in the northern part of the state, then visit the Central Valley, then go south, then back north, and, well, you get the idea. Everyone else is envious of our scenic route, especially the Midwest team. "Oh, goodie, a week in Wichita," says a slightly bitter Luke.

The only other highlight was getting our new, designer Wienermobile outfits—a hat, three pairs of khaki shorts, three T-shirts, three red polo shirts, a nylon flight suit, a yellow fleece, and a rain jacket—all embroidered with a cute Wienermobile logo. It's going to take another suitcase just to fit all this.

Adjusting to corporate culture has been a struggle for most of us. We strain to keep our eyes open during long, dry presentations. Imagine the shock when we opened out agendas and saw items like "Human Resources Forum," "Equity Overview," "Ethnic Marketing," "Issues Management," and "Discussion."

While I pinch myself to stay awake, Melissa has found an even better solution. "Where were you?" I ask when she returns to the conference room after a long absence.

"Oh, I took a nap in the bathroom," she answers matter-of-factly.

But today there's no need for napping. We're standing in the Oscar Mayer parking lot, staring at a pair of real, live Wienermobiles. On the right is the 1995 model, its surface shining like a thousand orange suns. On the left is the 1988 version, which looks not so good.

Although they're both shaped like hot dogs, the two vehicles couldn't be more different. The '95 is sleek and aerodynamic; the '88 is bulky and low to the ground. The '95 has bright, toasted yellow buns; the '88 is pasty and faded. The '95 has a metallic front grill that's shaped like a smile, the '88 has an asymmetrical "smile" hastily fashioned out of electrical tape. It's like comparing an F-18 to a biplane.

The '95 Wienermobile is an engineering marvel that was designed to command consumer attention, and it succeeds without question. From the oversized body to the pristine windows, this car will not be ignored. Don't even try to ignore it. You can't. Why are you trying? Accept it.

Russ walks us around the '95, showing off its hidden flourishes. Particularly cool are the Thunderbird headlights and a rear "watchdog" camera, mounted to make sure you don't back over any kids. Russ points out the large Oscar Mayer logo that is centered on the familiar yellow band.

"This is the Oscar Mayer rhomboid," Russ explains. "It's not a square, it's not a rectangle; it's a rhomboid." He turns the door key and the gull-wing door slowly swings up. It's hydraulic powered and very slow. We all stand around eagerly tapping our feet while waiting for the door to fully open. When it does, I shove my way to the front of the crowd and swiftly step inside.

A tour guide once told me, "I cannot explain beauty; I can only point it out." Well, the inside of this dog is beautiful. My eyes dart about, frantically trying to take it all in. There are green seats in front of me, green seats behind. I see yellows and reds, a hot dog–shaped dash, and cup holders! So many cup holders!

The cylindrical walls are covered with a gray, felt-like material that gives the main cabin (which is about six feet high) an artificial largeness. A "ketchup and mustard walkway" (actually a yellow stripe on red flooring) draws your eyes forward to the raised platform where the driver and shotgun (or "shotbun") passenger sit. The middle section is sunken and houses two captains' chairs and a gray cabinet for the TV/VCR/rudimentary stereo.

Twirling around, I notice another step up. This back platform holds two more chairs and a rather flimsy-looking closet door. I quickly count eight windows. Unless you crawl in the back or lie on your stomach, there's no hiding in this thing.

Russ allows us our moment of shock and awe. He then patiently points out all the features that make a Wienermobile a Wienermobile. To list a few:

* Ketchup-splattered carpet (actually black carpet with red fabric splotches)
* The bunroof (a clever name for the sunroof located near the front of the dog)
* Relish-colored seats (tastefully embroidered with miniature Wienermobiles)
* A rear closet (with storage for luggage and more than ten thousand Wiener Whistles)

Russ steps onto the front platform and claims "shotbun." One at a time, we file up and sit in the driver's seat. When it's my turn, I carefully lower myself into position. The commander's seat is plush and comfortable, like a well-worn recliner. I reach up and tentatively put both hands on the wheel. It feels good, like a steering wheel should. My grip tightens and joy takes over. Suddenly I'm a kid again, pretending that the family Cutlass is the General Lee.

As driver, the first thing you notice is perspective. With 180 degrees of glass, the view from the driver's seat is unobstructed and amazing. This is how hamsters must feel in those plastic balls. The dashboard and all the gauges are cleverly incorporated into a small, fiberglass hot dog. On the passenger's side, a similar hot dog serves as the glove compartment.

Russ quickly highlights the AM/FM radio, CB, and rearview monitor. There are controls for heat and air, although I've already been warned that these don't work ("It's not a chili dog," is the company line when we're asked about air-conditioning). Russ points up to a small black console attached to the ceiling. On the box are multicolored plastic switches labeled KETCHUP, MUSTARD, and RELISH.

"And these are the condiment dispensers," says Russ.

"What do they do?" I ask.

"Nothing," he deadpans. "They're just for show."

Having spent enough time in Wiener Wonderland, our tour group moves to the '88. Sadly, this is the model we'll be driving in California for the next few months. I guess the office figured that they couldn't give us the best territory *and* a modern Wienermobile.

I walk around the old dog, kick the tires, and take inventory. The '95 is spacious and welcoming; the '88 is cramped and confining. There are no side windows, so a dark gloom pervades the cabin. And unless you're Little Oscar, the low ceiling forces you to assume a permanent hunch. The experience is more like caving than commuting. The ketchup-splattered carpeting is here, as are the relish-colored seats. These seats, however, are narrower, and there's seating for only four. Gone is the entertainment center, several windows, and—gasp—the countless cup holders.

Joel, the newly appointed Hotdogger advisor (who just got off the road), beckons me from the passenger's seat. Slowly I make my way forward, head scraping against the ceiling. My path is soon blocked by a carpeted mountain—the engine cover. I look helplessly at Joel, unsure how to proceed.

"Just climb over the engine," he coaches. "And watch your feet."

Climb over the engine? What is this, Russia?!

To get into the seat without stepping on it, I have to face Joel, kneel on the engine cover, and then awkwardly lower my left leg to the floor. It's a long and painful stretch given that there's not much room down there. After a few seconds of flailing, I finally get my footing and tumble into the driver's seat.

While the '95 gives the driver plenty of room, the front of the '88 feels like a launch capsule. My thighs are pressed together, hot and sticky after the gymnastics routine. My left foot is pinned back at an odd angle while my right foot discovers that the gas and the brake pedals are so close that they should just be combined.

I check the enormous side-view mirror that is bolted onto the front of the Wienermobile. In it, I can see people laughing and smiling in the '95. They look so happy back there, with standing room and full circulation in their legs. For the first time in my life, I experience wiener envy.

After a few days of observing Sofia in the wild, I already feel as if I know her. She was born in Argentina, a fact that she's fiercely proud of. Despite the fact that she spent most of her life in Florida, she enjoys mentioning her South American heritage. In fact, Madison is the farthest north she's ever been. Sofia's second-round interview was the first time she'd ever seen snow. She likes mixed drinks; can't stand beer. She always eats healthy. She favors outfits that show off her slender shoulders; she doesn't own many T-shirts.

Every day I try to sit next to Sofia in Conference Room A. And every day I try to make her laugh. Sometimes it's by begging for Spanish lessons. Other times it's by offering to buy her dental coverage (which, under the generous Oscar Mayer health plan, is only $3 a month).

I look at Sofia as a puzzle that I have an entire year to figure out. If my track record with women is any indication, it'll take me at least that long. I love women, and I'm great at being friends with them, but relationships give me trouble. I'm the guy who blew off a date's birthday so I could play video games, the guy whose longest relationship was with a Mormon I saw only in the summers, the guy who got invited to a girl's lake house for the weekend and then made her cry by poking fun at her belly-button ring. My sad stories about women far outweigh my happy ones.

I want this to be my year to change that. A future plan *and* a Sofia, those are my goals.

"We're gonna leave and I'm still gonna have no idea how to drive that thing," says Hotdogger Melissa one day. She's not the only one who's nervous. We've stared at the Wienermobile, walked around the Wienermobile, and even sat in the Wienermobile, but there's been no talk of actually turning the key.

That's not to say we haven't spent a lot of time *talking* about driving. One exercise designed to get us ready for the Wienermobile was called "narrative driving."

"You've been driving five or six years and a lot of things happen unconsciously," Russ explains. "We want to make them conscious things." To do this, we each took turns driving a white passenger van and had to point out everything we saw, like "stop sign," "pothole," "Arby's." The lesson I took away from this exercise is that driving is really boring.

Our time recently has been spent learning about Share the Smiles, this year's Wienermobile campaign. It's replacing Talent Search, Oscar Mayer's popular search to find a child commercial star. Share the Smiles is Oscar Mayer's first attempt at mixing charity and the Wienermobile. Our job as Hotdoggers will be to travel to various events and collect money for local food banks. People can have a Polaroid picture taken with the Wienermobile for a suggested $1 donation. Not only do they get to keep the picture, we'll even put it in a flimsy paper frame. Big spenders willing to make a $5 donation get a plush Wienermobile beanbag toy ("Beanie Wienies").

Russ keeps mentioning "cause marketing" and explains that combating hunger is a natural fit for one of the world's largest food companies. I'm glad we'll be using the Wienermobile to achieve noble ends, but I wonder if this Share the Smiles idea came about as a way to deflect any anti-meat protestors. As I discovered during my second-round interview, some people are angry because they see the Wienermobile as a rolling billboard for meat consumption. Which is silly because the Wienermobile *is* a rolling billboard for meat consumption.

In case we encounter any hostile or uncomfortable situations when the press is around, we recently spent an afternoon going over "crisis communications." The trick is to deflect the question and steer the message toward what you want to talk about. The key phrase we're given is "I don't know about that, but what I do know is . . ." Here's how it would work in a hypothetical interview scenario.

Hypothetical reporter: "Can you explain how the Wienermobile ended up in a ditch?"

Me: "I don't know about that, but what I do know is that we're really excited to be in Bakersfield, California today!" Textbook deflection.

In between the quizzes and the PR training and the hour-long discussion on when it's appropriate to wear shorts, Hotdoggers XII has found time to bond. Russ almost commands it by his insistence on eating together every night. The forced togetherness has been fun and enlightening. Every day you learn something new about your fellow Hotdoggers. For instance, I had no idea that wanting to drive the Wienermobile could cause so much family conflict. I mean, my parents were all for it.

"I was super excited, but my parents were not," Leah tells us one night over drinks. It seems her family thought it was a joke. They didn't believe it was a real job and insisted it was a really bad idea to not take the corporate Eli Lilly job she'd been offered.

"How did you convince them?" I ask.

"I didn't really. I just took the job."

"Yeah, my parents weren't too into it either," says Debbie.

Candace joins the conversation and offers perhaps the best parental reaction. "Well, my mom was terrified. She thought for sure I was going to have to wear a hot dog costume."

CHAPTER 7

ust when we're all about to give up on actually driving a Wienermobile, Russ announces that today is the day. We're taking the Wienermobile . . . around the parking lot.

Russ stands outside one of the '88s. "Are you ready to do some driving, Mr. Ihlenfeld?"

"Yes, sir."

Russ hands me the keys and heads inside. My partners, Ali and Sofia, follow him in. In little under a week, our team has developed a respectful, businesslike relationship.

"Don't kill us," Ali says to me.

Ali and Sofia giggle like schoolgirls in the backseat, already the best of friends. It's a little annoying since I want to be Sofia's best friend.

The ladies buckle up while I once again try to summit the engine block. Russ watches like an angry hawk, making certain that I don't step on the seat. If there's one rule with the '88 Wienermobile it's "don't step on the seat." After some twists that would make a ballerina blush, I'm behind the wheel and ready to begin the rest of my life.

"Start her up," commands Russ.

I turn the key and the Wienermobile purrs to life. It's a loud, wonderful sound. This vehicle feels powerful, although that may be because

I'm sitting next to the engine. My arms vibrate as I grip the steering wheel tight.

"Whenever you're ready," says Russ. "Just go slow and be sure to check your mirrors."

I dutifully check the side mirrors and notice nothing but a sea of asphalt. My right hand grabs the gearshift and yanks down. My foot eases off the brake and the Wienermobile lurches forward, as if trying to escape the lot.

The Wienermobile handles surprisingly well considering its length and girth. I feel like I'm driving the world's biggest minivan. The most challenging consideration is spatial orientation. In the '88, the driver's seat is positioned a few feet in front of the front tires, so it's hard to know how much room you have up front.

Russ motions to a parking spot in the distance. "Why don't you pull into that spot?"

Cautiously, I approach the target. I really wish someone were out on the tarmac waving me in. I crawl forward, aiming for the concrete bumper stop. My buns spill over the yellow lines and I quickly learn that it's impossible to squeeze a Wienermobile into a standard parking spot.

"I don't think we're going to fit," I say.

"Just keep pulling forward," says Russ.

The bumper stop is now somewhere under my feet.

"Should I be stopping?"

"Just a bit farther. Go slowly," says Russ.

And then THUMP—I hit the concrete block.

"Not that far," says Russ.

Backing up the Wienermobile is a different dilemma. The '88 is missing a camera, so there's no telling what's behind you. I put it in reverse and instinctively look over my right shoulder. Ali and Sofia stare blankly back at me.

"I would just use the side mirrors," says Russ.

Things go much more smoothly after that. A few twirls around the lot and I already feel like an expert dog driver. I can't wait to get this thing up to highway speeds.

I pass the keys to Ali. "Now that's how you drive a Wienermobile."

"Yeah, really impressive," she says in her patented deadpan.

I move to the back. My legs are cramped and I'm drenched in sweat, but my spirits are high. I just drove the Oscar Mayer Wienermobile.

A few days later, it's me, Ali, Russ, and an '88—but for real this time. Two new Wienermobile drivers are about to be unleashed on the unsuspecting streets of Madison. It's a dangerous time to be a pedestrian.

Sadly, Sofia has already finished her driver's ed for the day and won't be joining us.

"How was it?" I ask her in passing.

"Terrifying at first. But then I got the hang of it."

"That's encouraging," I said. I then see Shawna, who's usually quite calm under pressure. "How was it, Shawna?"

"I was more nervous doing that than learning how to drive for the very first time," she says while wiping away some residual sweat. "Good luck, Hot Dog Dave."

Jamila, who took the job solely because she wanted to drive a cool car, is a bit more enthusiastic. "It's so powerful!" she gushes.

As I get behind the wheel, I can understand why Sofia and Shawna felt some trepidation—this is a lot of pressure. I turn the key, drive past the gate, and gently coast the '88 beyond the safe confines of the Oscar Mayer lot. Suddenly I'm solely responsible for the most expensive piece of machinery I'll ever operate. One wrong turn and I could doom the entire program. These must be the same butterflies Neil Armstrong felt.

I pull out of the lot slowly, speedometer hovering between 5 and 10 mph, and make a left on Mayer Avenue. Russ then tells me to turn right on Packers Avenue. Some very creative street names in Madison.

Russ's only advice at the onset is to "take it slow." And so I do, making very deliberate turns and keeping the Wienermobile around 15 mph. Russ may have overprepared us for driving, but he did little to ready us for the instant celebrity that comes with being a Hotdogger. To the outside world, seeing a Wienermobile is a big deal. I don't realize how big until I actually merge into traffic. Suddenly all eyes are on us, with people staring and honking and waving at this sausage-shaped apparition. I want to be a friendly ambassador, but I'm too petrified to wave back.

I soon discover another difficulty of driving in the real world—lanes. This beast is wide, and it's difficult to keep the Wienermobile from spilling into a second lane. It's also hard to look straight ahead *and* watch your buns in the mirror. Inevitably, I drift a bit. Soon, I brush against the curb and then smack into a pothole—an inauspicious start to my career.

"Just try to stay in the center," says Russ.

Yeah, like that's possible.

I see a stop sign in the distance. Finally, something I know how to do. I tap the pedal and the Wienermobile slows . . . barely. Next to me, Russ starts to squirm. The stop sign comes up so fast that I have to slam the brake pedal, jolting the Wienermobile (and its occupants) to a very ungraceful stop.

I cautiously peek over at Russ, who's busy digging the seat belt out of his chest cavity. "Try not to stop so fast," he says. "You'll give your partners whiplash."

"Yeah, Dave. I have a delicate neck," says Ali.

"It looks pretty sturdy to me," I reply.

"Are you calling me fat?" she says in mock anger.

Russ quickly refocuses us on our task. "Let's get back to driving, please. Hands at ten and two."

Soon my heart rate returns to pre-cardiac arrest and I start to actually enjoy the experience. People wave and I tentatively raise some fingers to return the greeting. Russ leans back in his chair, nails no longer digging into the upholstery.

My trepidation about this job has slowly been eroded during Hot Dog High. It's helped that I've met so many fascinating new friends (especially Sofia), but actually driving the Oscar Mayer Wienermobile has put me over the top. That's it, I've swallowed the magic pill, I've downed the Kool-Aid, I've joined the cult. I'm a Hotdogger and proud of it.

Eventually Russ points to the curb ahead. "Why don't you pull over here and we'll let Ali drive."

But I wanna go again! I think. With heavy heart, I bring the Wienermobile to a relatively gentle stop and climb to the back.

I push past Ali as we swap positions. "Try not to kill us," I say.

"Please. You're in for the ride of your life." Ali flashes a devilish smile before climbing into the driver's seat. "Okay, Russ, let's do this!"

While Ali is a decent enough driver, she's no Hot Dog Dave. After only a few minutes behind the wheel, a tense Russ is already glaring at her. Ali is perhaps a bit too enthusiastic, waving at every car, bus, and pedestrian we pass. She thrusts her left arm out the window and wildly flaps it about. The girl is going to dislocate something.

Russ shakes his head. "Maybe focus more on the road until you're comfortable."

Ali sadly pulls her arm back into the Wienermobile and plops it onto the steering wheel. It takes an enormous amount of willpower to stop her waving.

While I'm a bit nervous about Ali the driver, I really enjoy Ali the person. She isn't shy about using her charm but is hardly limited to niceties. What lies beneath her sweet façade is a truly sarcastic soul. People often complain that it's hard to tell if I'm serious or joking. Ali is the exact same way.

This is why I assume Ali is joking when she looks to Russ and says, "The temperature needle's red. Is that bad?" Turns out, she's serious.

"Hmmm, might have to pull over for a bit," says Russ after a thoughtful examination of the temperature gauge.

We're close to the InnTowner, our Madison hotel, and seek refuge in the hotel's parking lot. Wiener wheezing, wisps of smoke wafting from under the buns, we limp to the finish line. Sitting behind the engine, I can tell you that it's radiating pure, white heat. The cabin feels like a sauna.

Ever the calm general, Russ embraces the situation. "This will be a good time to learn about coolant."

Russ gathers us near the door and then yanks up the engine cover, releasing a new wave of warmth. We all step back to avoid melting.

We've been warned that the Wienermobile has a tendency to overheat. Turns out, "tendency" is the wrong word. The Wienermobile has a "need" to overheat. Even the slightest incline will pin the temperature needle. The only tip offered to deal with this problem is to drive with the heat on. It's an ironic solution at best.

Russ pours a few gallons of blue coolant into the engine. "And now we wait."

"How long does it take to cool down?" asks Ali.

"About thirty minutes," responds Russ. "Sometimes an hour."

An hour? My thoughts drift to the practical. If the Wienermobile can't handle the gentle, practically nonexistent slopes of Madison, what's going to happen in the mountains of California? Did anyone consider that before sending us off to certain death?

Eventually the car cools and we head to Penske to get our ailing dog checked out. This time, Ali doesn't even want to wave.

For those who have never been long haul truckers, Penske may be unfamiliar. The company, started by auto racer Roger Penske, does everything from truck rental to transportation logistics (whatever that is). The division we'll be dealing with is automotive repair.

Penske has shops all across the country and a twenty-four-hour hotline that we're supposed to call if we find ourselves stranded. It's like AAA on steroids.

The Madison Penske has obviously seen a lot of Wienermobile breakdowns. We pull in and a manager hurries out to check on the patient. Russ gives him the vital information and then a Penske van drops us off back at headquarters.

This is our first visit to Penske. Something tells me it won't be our last.

CHAPTER 8

Hot Dog High is almost over and I'm amazed at how close our group has grown. We've barbequed at Russ's suburban estate, eaten loads of free food, and gone through obscene amounts of alcohol. Well, I've gone through obscene amounts of alcohol.

The other night we were all at a local Madison pub, the Rathskeller. Looming over our happy family are the Outsiders—better known as Hotdoggers XI. It seems that, every year, the previous year's team ends their tenure by swinging through Madison for a grand send-off.

Hotdoggers XI blow into town in a tornado of hugs and handshakes. I struggle to keep the names straight—there's Kristy and Burke and Alex and a few names that start with M. Everyone appears happy, healthy, and only slightly exhausted.

These Hotdoggers went through the same training as us, but they couldn't be more different. "They're so confident," says Debbie. "Who are they? Why are they so cool?"

Eight people from Hotdoggers XI will be staying and joining our group. These veterans were hired in December (when Oscar Mayer realized they needed more people for Share the Smiles) and have been on the road since February. They'll be with us until the Share the Smiles finale in November. Our new partner, Brad, will be joining us for a few months on Team California. It's not often that a veteran gets teamed with three virgins (Wienermobile virgins, that is), but I suppose the office wants to ensure a seamless Share the Smiles transition.

Brad has been on the road for eight months. I've talked with him on the phone a few times and he seems like a nice enough guy. But I'm leery of any new elements that might disrupt our team's embryonic chemistry. Also, I want him to stay away from Sofia. I hope he has a thing for opinionated blondes.

From across the room comes a deep, twangy shout. "There's my team!" Turning around, I spot a guy swaggering toward Ali, Sofia, and me. This must be him.

Brad moves with a confidence born from being both tall and lean. Even from a distance, he gives off a rugged charm. The only thing keeping him out of Marlboro ads is his preppy sweater vest and male pattern baldness.

Brad swings his whole body into a handshake. "Dave! Buddy! How's it going?" he says through a narrow, devilish smile.

"Fine?" I say, struggling to match his tone and volume.

Brad then offers the same firm handshake to Sofia and Ali. The girls are immediately smitten.

Being from Texas, Brad has a drawl. But unlike most drawls, Brad's is fast and smooth. "You guys ready to hit the road? Because we could go now. Got my stuff 'round back."

The girls can't help but laugh while I just stand and smile awkwardly. My antennae are up with this guy. He just seems too funny, too sure, too . . . Brad.

The next morning, Russ gathers everyone together in the hotel banquet hall so we can bid farewell to Hotdoggers XI. We first go around the room so everyone can explain what they're doing next. Surprisingly, very few have any sort of plan. Even more surprising, no one seems worried about it. I hope that's me in a year.

Russ then retakes center stage to give his closing address. "When you take this job, you give up your life, your friends, and your family. You're on the road for a year and it's not easy," he says. "But I don't think you'll ever forget the experiences you have out there or the friends you make in here. Thanks for all you do."

There's a lot of emotion in the room as Hotdoggers XI say their good-byes. Even the men openly weep. It may sound harsh, but I'm excited about their exit.

It's our sausage now.

The next few days are occupied by more training and some intensive team building. We climb ropes, jump off lofty poles, and generally practice trusting each other. In very short order, Brad emerges as the leader of our little group. It's not like he campaigned for the job; he just won it by default. The rest of us don't know what it's like out there on the cold, lonely highways. Brad does.

Another reason Brad's the leader is that he has a way with words. The man is full of stories, advice, anecdotes, jokes, recipes . . . you name it. And he's definitely not afraid of sharing his thoughts.

Brad, on driving a Wienermobile: "Take a real wide turn. I had driven this crappy car of my Dad's, it was like a Delta '88 Oldsmobile. It was like the same size of the '88 Wienermobile. That's it—go farther than you need to and turn wider than you need to."

Brad, on how he got through Hot Dog High: "You just shut up for forty hours a week for two weeks knowing that they're going to give you the keys so you can go goof off."

Predictably, Russ has a slightly different outlook on Hot Dog High. When we started, he told us, "You don't know what you don't know." On our last day, he brings us together and says, "Now you know what you don't know. Learn the rest."

And with that, he hands us the keys.

CHAPTER 9

From the beginning, Oscar F. Mayer understood the importance of marketing. The company sponsored polka bands around Chicago, as well as the German Exposition at the 1893 Chicago World's Fair. The Mayers went to great lengths to make sure consumers knew their name.

An article in Retail Merchandiser explains an early part of Oscar's strategy: "As the fame of their product grew, the Mayers feared other meat packers might try to capitalize on their popularity. So in 1904, when some of the largest packing houses were still selling their own meats anonymously, the Mayers took the bold step of affixing a brand name to their products. Oscar Mayer, the brand, was born."

The company started using the name "Edelweiss" (a type of German flower) on products such as bacon and linked sausage. Soon, delivery trucks stamped with the new brand were making deliveries in and around Chicago.

In 1906, Oscar Mayer became "one of the first companies to receive the safety seal from the newly created Food Safety Inspection Service." Hot dog historian Bruce Kraig points out the importance of this push toward purity. "This idea of purity of food grew up as early as the 1870s. After the Pure Food and Drug Act of 1906, that became paramount in advertising. Oscar realized that if he said his product was superior to all others, and he pushed that, it would create sales. And it did."

As sales expanded, more money was allocated for advertising. In 1915, the company spent $2,000 for a window display. In 1917, Oscar Mayer became the first meat packer to advertise in the newspaper.

These 1917 ads may seem quaint now, but they were revolutionary at the time. One that appeared in the Chicago Daily Tribune on August 26, 1917, proclaimed: "Reduce Your Meat Bills!! Serve More Sausage" and went on to say "Here's an idea for the alert housewife. Serve Oscar Mayer's Sausages. Solid meat! No bone! No extra fat! No waste! 100% fine food."

A Chicago Daily Tribune ad from April 1, 1917, read: "Oscar Mayer's meat delicacies are famous everywhere for unusual flavor and purity. Government Inspected for Your Protection."

Oscar Mayer dropped the Edelweiss name in 1918 and began stamping products with "Oscar Mayer Approved Meat Products." The company continued its expansion, buying a meat packing plant in Madison, Wisconsin, in 1919. This location would become Oscar Mayer headquarters in 1957.

Perhaps the most revolutionary marketing coup occurred in 1929 when Oscar Mayer & Co. became the first meat producers to brand their wieners with a paper band. The yellow band appeared on every fourth hot dog and bore the Oscar Mayer name in red along with a U.S. government inspection stamp. The bands were applied by hand until 1944, when machinery automated the process.

It's difficult to underestimate the importance of the yellow band. "The Yellow Band Label singled out the brand," writes Kraig. "Red and yellow became the iconic colors for hot dogs, for other companies and hot dog sellers alike." Oscar G. Mayer Jr. said that the band opened the way for advertising "unheard of for meat products at the time." One of the company's earliest slogans was: "Look for the brand with the yellow band. Oh so fresh, oh so grand."

"They had a keen eye on how to market their product," says Kraig. "It was all about visibility and purity."

CHAPTER 10

June 20, 1999—my first official day on the road. It's time to test these fragile wings of bologna.

Having been delayed by a friend's wedding in St. Louis (where the only question asked was "Are you really driving the Wienermobile?!"), I join Team California a few days late. We rendezvous at a Holiday Inn in Stockton, a small town in Northern California that is almost completely without scenery. The view from my hotel room includes a taco stand, the ruins of a park, and a power plant that wafts thick black smoke into the sky. When people think of sunny California, they don't think of this place.

My teammates have just finished working two days at the San Joaquin County Fair and look exhausted when they finally make it back to the hotel.

"Daveeeeee!" screeches Sofia as she comes into my room. She rushes over and gives me an extended hug. Her hair is pressed against my face and I take in the scent, a mixture of perfume and cotton candy. On her it works.

Turning around, I see Ali. "Hello, David," she says in a slightly teasing tenor. Of course, we have to hug as well.

Brad soon makes his grand entrance. "Well, look who decided to join us! Glad you could make it, young David." Brad and I shake hands, not quite ready for a hug.

"How was the fair?" I ask.

"Eh," replies Sofia as she plops down on my bed.

"Dave, let me tell you, it was fantastic," says Brad. "You missed a good time."

"You didn't miss anything," says Ali.

"Quiet, Ali. Don't tell him what he did or did not miss," says Brad.

Already I sense some comedic tension among the group. Brad takes great pleasure in playfully relating all the "mistakes" Ali has made so far. Like how he had to steer the Wienermobile out of LA because he couldn't put up with Ali's driving.

"And listen to this," Brad continues. "So, yesterday, I show up early to Ali's room and she literally just got out of bed."

"I was up!"

"Mind you, it's pretty easy to wake up in hotels," he continues. "Pretty easy to call and get a wake-up call. There's also the alarm clock. I have to wait thirty minutes for her to get ready. Ali was late for her first day on the job."

"Oh, like you're Mr. Punctuality," retorts Ali.

"Hey, if you're on time you're late," says a beaming Brad, repeating one of Russ's favorite phrases.

"Brad, be nice," says Sofia. And like a chastised puppy, Brad stops barking.

The next morning we're scheduled to make the eighty-two-mile trip from Stockton to San Francisco and I try to make up for my absence. "I can drive," I offer.

"Great," Sofia says.

"Fantastic," Ali replies.

"Knock yourself out," Brad scoffs.

Two days in and my teammates have lost all enthusiasm for driving the '88. They are, however, very excited about our rental car, a shiny

Ford Mustang. Why do we have a rental car when our job is to drive a mobile hot dog? Let me explain.

Oscar Mayer is not into the Wienermobile to lose money. We get $60 a night for hotels and $20 a day for food. Most people would go cold and hungry on a budget like that. But while we're not pampered, the Wienermobile certainly is.

Every night, we're supposed to keep the Wienermobile secure by leaving it at the fairgrounds or the nearest Penske. Since we need a way to get back to our hotel, Russ has authorized every team to get a rental car. Here's the amazing part: we can keep the rental car for as long as we're in one area. The only thing we can't do is drive a rental car up and down the state; that's what the Wienermobile is for.

"I call the Mustang!" says Ali after she tosses her mammoth luggage bag in the back of the Wienermobile.

"Aw, not fair, I want the Mustang," says Sofia.

Brad holds up the rental car keys. "Well, I'm driving so one of you get in."

Ali and Sofia gamely stare each other down. "Rock-paper-scissors?" suggests Ali.

"Rock-paper-scissors," agrees Sofia.

It seems Team California has already worked out a fair and efficient system for settling disputes. Two rocks and a scissors later, Ali is the victor. "Have fun in the '88!" she shouts while skipping to the rental car.

I soon find out why there was such a fight over the Mustang. Hot Dog High only hints at how uncomfortable a Wienermobile can be. To get the full taste, you need to spend a few hours in the thing. With no air-conditioning and plenty of incoming sunlight, the Wienermobile instantly becomes a sauna. A vent on the driver's side floor blows a steady stream of hot air onto my bare legs.

We've been assigned a hobbled '88 Wienermobile with the license plate HOTDOGG'N. This thing is a horror show on wheels, but I try to put the pain aside and focus on flirting with Sofia. She's riding shotbun for our trip north, and I take the opportunity to ask about what I missed.

"Not much," she says. "Just took a lot of pictures, passed out a *ton* of whistles."

"People seem to like the whistles."

"I know! They always come up and ask for, like, ten. One for their kids, one for their grandbabies . . ."

"Grandbabies?"

Sofia laughs knowingly. "You'll see."

"Team getting along?"

"Oh, yeah, we've been having a great time," she says. "Brad's so funny."

I knew giving that guy a two-day head start would come back to haunt me. "He hasn't been bossing you guys around too much?" I ask in a hopeful tone.

"What? No, it's been fun."

"Cool. Yeah, he seems like a good guy."

"Yeah," agrees Sofia.

Sofia soon returns to reading her thick fashion magazine while I take us through the vast nothingness that is Central California. For miles the only thing we pass are farm fields and fruit stands. This is not the land of surf and palm trees; this is the land of dirt and irrigation.

"Do you want me to drive?" asks Sofia, snapping me out of my driving trance.

"No, that's okay. I've got it."

"Okay . . . well I'm going to take a nap in the back. Just let me know if you get tired."

"Oh . . . okay."

With that, Sofia climbs over the engine cover and plops down in the slight shade of our collected luggage. Love will have to wait a few more exits.

First stop is Vacaville, an agricultural town located midway between Sacramento and San Francisco. Vacaville (Spanish for "Cowville") is not the prettiest place in California. The scenery is more brown than green, with an occasional rolling hill to break up the monotonous flatness. There's a lot of land and not a lot of people, although the outlet mall appears busy.

My inaugural Wienermobile event, a three-hour supermarket stop, is not glamorous, but everything's exciting your first time.

A nervous anticipation fills my stomach as I drive the Wienermobile into a sprawling strip mall parking lot that is already packed with early morning shoppers. To avoid moving vehicles and gawking pedestrians, I'm forced to take a somewhat circuitous route. It's down one row, then a sharp left, then down another row, then a right. Each turn of the wheel is slow and deliberate.

That's it . . . easy now . . .

Miraculously, I make it to the front of the store without any casualties or vehicular damage. Brad goes to greet the store manager. You can tell he's the store manager because he's the only one wearing a tie. And because he can't stop smiling. Brad gets instructions from the man and then guides me into our storefront spot. Outside my window, a crowd of curious shoppers is already forming.

"Give us a minute, please," I overhear Brad telling the onlookers. "We'll be with you soon!"

Brad quickly asserts himself as we unload the vehicle. "Dave, can you grab the donation box? Ali, why don't you empty some whistle boxes?" he orders. "Sofia, I'll help you with the table." The three of us flutter about like worker bees trying to impress the queen.

The nice thing about Share the Smiles is that you could train a monkey to do it. The setup is quick and painless: a folding table, a blue tablemat, a donation box, one Polaroid camera, some boxes of film, a few decorative frames, and a bag full of whistles.

The pitch is even easier: "Hello, would you like to get your picture taken with the Oscar Mayer Wienermobile? It's just a dollar donation to your local food bank."

I get ignored the first few times I try to solicit customers. "Hello, would you like to get your picture taken with—"

But before I can finish, a woman interrupts. "I was just wondering if I could get one of those whistles."

"Oh, sure," I say, reaching deep into the bag and handing over a plastic toy. "Would you like to donate—"

"Actually, could I get three more for my grandbabies?"

Ah, those grandbabies. Sofia wasn't lying.

Not many people want to donate, or even hear the pitch, after they see the free whistles. Thoughts of handing over an empty donation envelope to the food bank cross my mind. "Should I be doing something different?" I ask Brad.

"Nah. People either give or they don't."

As usual, Brad knows of what he speaks. Eventually, money starts filling the donation box and soon we've got a line of people waiting to get their pictures taken with the world-famous Wienermobile.

Share the Smiles comes with some defined roles. Besides the greeter and the picture taker, there's the framer, the person who must deftly tuck the Polaroid into its commemorative cardboard frame. We take turns rotating through the various positions, although it's rare that everyone is doing actual work.

"I'm going for some water," says Brad as he heads inside the store.

"I'm going to book our hotels," says Sofia as she heads toward the pay phone.

I saunter over to Ali, who's happily handing out whistles. "Do we get a lot of breaks?"

"As many as you want."

"Why don't you take one?"

"I don't know . . . I like passing out whistles."

I don't indulge in many breaks either, preferring to just silently scowl whenever a teammate takes one. Besides, I'm having too much fun watching people watch the Wienermobile.

This being a weekday morning, the crowd is mostly moms and their young children. Occasionally we'll get an office worker on lunch or a truck driver making his scheduled delivery. But no matter the demographic, the questions are the same. Now I understand why we spent so much time memorizing puns at Hot Dog High.

"How fast does it go?" *It hauls buns!*

"Do you sleep in that thing?" *No, it's not a Wienie-bago.*

"How did you get the job?" *I cut the mustard.*

"Does it have air-conditioning?" *It's not a chili dog.*

"What does it run on?" *High-octane mustard.*

"How does it handle?" *It's very aero-dog-namic.*

"What's it built on?" *A GMC Dually truck chassis.*

"Can I go inside?" *No.*

Vacaville loves the Wienermobile. Even the store's meat manager comes out to survey the scene and is impressed with the increased traffic. "So this is why all my hot dogs are going!" he says in amazement.

For three hours, puns fly and flashes flash. We take more than two hundred pictures, raise a good amount for the food bank, push plenty of Oscar Mayer product, and, most importantly, make a lot of people happy.

I no longer envy all my friends who had master plans and are now stuck in soulless cubicles, staring at the clock and breathlessly waiting for their next coffee break.

All in all, not a bad first day of work.

CHAPTER 11

Never in my life did I think I would be attending the Alameda County Fair in Pleasanton, California, let alone working it. But here I am, standing on a small patch of grass in front of the Wienermobile, kindly trying to solicit donations from complete strangers.

A husband and wife walk by. He's holding her hand and she's holding a tower of cotton candy. They look like the perfect marks. "Would you like to have your picture taken with the Oscar Mayer Wienermobile? It's only a dollar donation to your local food bank."

The couple walks by without making eye contact.

"You've got to put some backbone into it," suggests Brad. "Here, watch."

Another couple, this one a bit younger, enters our area. Brad gets out from behind the booth and practically blocks their path. "Hello folks! Welcome to the Wienermobile! We're here at the fair today collecting donations for your local food bank. Just a dollar donation and you can have your picture taken with the Wienermobile. We'll even toss in a commemorative frame for free."

The couple seems dumbfounded by the awesomeness of the offer. "Uh, sure, sounds good," says the man.

"Fantastic, you won't regret it!" barks Brad. "Just put your donation in the box and step in front of the giant hot dog."

It really is something to watch him work.

The theme of the Alameda County Fair is "The Gold Rush Is On," but not many people seem interested in panning. Attendance is way down because last Fourth of July a gunman sprayed bullets at the midway crowd, hitting eight people who were waiting to get into a Peter Frampton concert (this we find out not from Russ, but from the woman in charge of the camel rides). In response, there are now metal detectors at the gates. It's not the most festive fair environment, but they are offering concerts by Sister Sledge and Rick Springfield.

We're stationed right next to the livestock pavilion, which makes for all sorts of interesting aromas. Despite the stench, the Wienermobile proves to be quite a draw, especially once people discover the free whistles.

A common customer interaction goes something like this:

"What are you all giving away today?"

"Well, you can take a Wiener Whistle . . ."

"Can I have two more?"

"Sure. Here you go. We're also—"

"What else you got?"

"Well, you can get your picture taken for a dollar donation to your local food bank."

Blank stare. "Can I go inside?"

"No, sorry. You can peek in the windows, though."

Another blank stare. Some chin scratching. "Can I get a few more of those whistles?"

During a lull in the action, I walk over to Brad. "Some of these people are crazy."

"Yeah, but you'll get used to 'em."

Ali walks over with a confused look on her face. "A man came up to me and told me his life story. How he married a forty-year-old woman and she was heading back to Mexico to take care of her mother who was having her leg amputated." Ali pauses, letting all this sink in. "So that's been my day."

Sofia returns from wherever she wandered off to. "I booked our next three hotels," she says. "Oh, and I'm waiting to hear back about staying at a condo on Lake Tahoe."

A few hours into our shift and I think I'm getting the hang of this. I figure out the best way to frame a Wienermobile photo (stand near the front, not the side), how to quickly develop a Polaroid picture (shake, don't blow), and what Sofia's favorite fair food is (kettle corn).

I object to those who think this isn't a real job. *You* try smiling and being polite for five hours—it's not easy. By the end of our shift, it's a struggle to take pictures and even harder to continue talking in pun-speak. We're exhausted and ready for our freshly made beds and free HBO.

As we're packing up for the night, a kid spots our Wienermobile and pulls his weary mom over for a closer look. "This is so cool!" he shouts. I know exactly what he's talking about.

This job is odd in so many ways. But what I still can't believe is that there's really no adult supervision. Sure, we have to show up to our events and e-mail reports every night, but no one is physically cracking the whip. So Sofia is totally free to take hour-long lunches with Brad. The only repercussion is a disapproving glare from me.

Despite our strange job, we keep a somewhat normal schedule— five days on, two days off, except our off days are rarely Saturday and Sunday. Those are prime fair days. Off days are completely our own, and having a rental car gives us some range. Russ encourages the teams to take advantage of their locations. "Get out, see, explore," he told us at Hot Dog High.

So far we've spent most of our off time in the Bay Area. "They must have painted the Golden Gate Bridge," said a slightly confused Ali as we drove over the battleship gray Bay Bridge.

We've hiked the hilly streets of San Francisco, taken a boat cruise around Alcatraz, and toured Muir Woods. Well, actually, I drove us through Muir Woods with my nap-happy teammates passed out in the back. It was not the bonding experience I had hoped for.

Besides work days and off days, there are also drive days. Today is one of those days. This is where the office allots an entire day to get from Point A to Point B. So far our drives have been short and not-so-sweaty. This is our first marathon journey—a 253-mile trek from Pleasanton to Rancho Cucamonga.

Brad is chosen to pilot the Wienermobile through our most treacherous terrain yet—a 4,183-foot climb through the dreaded Tehachapi pass.

HOTDOGG'N hates mountains, especially the going up part. Unfortunately, to get from Northern to Southern California on I-5 you must go through the fifty-mile Tehachapi Pass.

Starting our ascent, I notice some rather ominous highway signs:

WATER, 1 MILE AHEAD

TEST BRAKES

TURN OFF AIR CONDITIONER

As we climb, so too does the temperature needle—inching toward the critical red zone. The hot, sticky air mixes with a thick sense of worry to create a very hostile work environment.

Brad has the gas pedal pushed practically *through* the floor, but this is the little engine that can't. We continue to chug along at an embarrassing rate. Another mile and the needle's pinned in the red. A sick smell, like burning tires smothered in rotten bananas, creeps through the cabin. Brad sees an exit sign reading FORT TEJON and decides it's time to pull over. We stop in the small parking lot and burst out of the vehicle, desperate for fresh air. With an hour before the Wienermobile is fit to drive again, there's nothing to do but tour the grounds.

"I don't know," says a skeptical Sofia. "It looks educational."

Turns out Fort Tejon is a pretty interesting place. It was used before and after the Civil War and has been restored by the Park Service. We walk into the general's residence and are met by Park Ranger Sean.

"Oh, hello," he says, seemingly caught off guard by the presence of actual visitors. But once he gets over the shock of seeing people, Sean proves to be very informative. He tells us of the fort's ill-fated camel corps, a 1930s Army experiment to see if camels could be used in the Southwest. Turns out they couldn't. In the end, the camels weren't any better than the horses or donkeys. So the Army eventually auctioned them off.

Despite the failure, some civic groups have attempted to inflate the camel legend. "It's stupid," says Sean. "They're just camels."

But that doesn't stop us from asking Sean a lot of questions about the camels:

"How long were they here?"

"How did they get them here?"

"Did the Army ever kill a camel?"

It feels nice to be the ones asking, rather than answering, inane questions for a change. We left Pleasanton at 10 a.m. and get into Rancho Cucamonga at 10 p.m. Twelve hours to go 253 miles. Not exactly hauling buns.

CHAPTER 12

*A*ll right, as soon as I park, you guys open the door and we all run to the store."

It sounds like the beginning to a really lame fairy tale, but it's actually Brad's plan for getting into Walmart undetected. We're not working at the store, just here to pick up a few travel essentials—sunscreen, bottled water, some new socks. Still, the Wienermobile attracts attention wherever it goes. Getting gas is an hour-long event, and there's no such thing as a "quick meal" when you pull up to a restaurant in the Wienermobile. We've even had cars trail us on the highway for an hour just so they could look inside when we finally pulled over.

Yes, it's a hassle at times, but I kind of enjoy the celebrity aspect. No one has ever paid this much attention to me before. Brad, however, is over it.

"Really? Do we have to run?" I ask.

"You can walk if you want. Just be prepared."

"I'm going to run," says Sofia.

"Yeah, me, too," says Ali.

"Okay, you guys have fun. I'll walk," I say.

Brad isn't serious about much, but he's very focused on this

Walmart mission. He pulls the Wienermobile into the farthest corner of the parking lot and shuts off the engine.

"Okay, let's go!" he shouts. Brad tosses me the keys and then I watch my team bolt out of the Wienermobile and sprint a good hundred yards to the front entrance.

Well, that's not very professional, I think.

In no hurry, I calmly lock up the Wienermobile and start toward the store.

"Hello! Hello!" comes a faint, female cry. I look over and spot a woman dragging her young child toward me.

"Yes?"

"Do you have any whistles?"

"Oh, sure. Let me get one."

I open up the Wienermobile, grab a few whistles, and hand them to the woman.

"Can I get a few more for my other kids?"

"Sure, not a problem," I say as I dive back into the whistle bag.

"Thank you so much!" The woman then leads her unimpressed child away. "This is a Wiener Whistle. Mommy had one when she was a little girl."

I once again lock up the Wienermobile and once again start toward the store. About halfway to the front door, an elderly man, his silver hair shining in the sun, unexpectedly pops out from behind the cart corral. "Excuse me!"

"Ahh!" I stammer.

"Do you drive that thing?" he asks while pointing back to the Wienermobile.

"I do."

"I can't believe it! I've been trying to get a Wienie Whistle for thirty years!"

"Oh, okay. Let me go back and get one."

Deep breath, Dave. Don't freak out here. These people sort of pay your salary. Sort of.

I turn around and trudge back to the Wienermobile. "Actually, could you make it three?!" shouts the old man.

The Wiener Whistle is an iconic creation, and being a Hotdogger means passing out hundreds of these cheap plastic toys each day. Running out of Wiener Whistles is like running out of oxygen—you die quickly.

The whistles made their debut in 1951. They were about two inches long and looked just like miniature bright orange hot dogs. The whistles featured the yellow Oscar Mayer band in the middle and had a variety of holes that could be covered and uncovered to create different musical notes. With some practice, it was even possible to play the Oscar Mayer jingle.

Wiener Whistles were an enormous success. They were handed out at events by Oscar Mayer's diminutive mascot, Little Oscar, and, starting in 1958, were even attached to packages of hot dogs. At the New York World's Fair in 1964, visitors could buy Wiener Whistles from a vending machine for two cents each.

The whistles were produced until 1971 and then replaced with Little Oscar Rings. The rings were yellow and red and featured the cartoon head of Little Oscar wearing a hot dog–shaped chef's hat.

When the Wienermobile was reintroduced in 1988, the most asked question was "Where are the Wiener Whistles?" According to former sales manager Tom Phillips, "The request for Wiener Whistles became so great that we started to find a manufacturer or someone who would give us an idea of what we could use for a Wiener Whistle that would satisfy the needs and wants of the consumers and still meet the needs of the child safety regulations."

Tom contacted four engineering companies and told them he had a fun little project for them to work on—redesign the Wiener Whistle so it could be safely passed out again. One of the companies took a stab at the problem and sent back what would become the updated Wiener Whistle.

The redesigned whistle was similar to the classic model. There were still plenty of holes and, with practice, it was still possible to play the jingle. The whistle was supposed to resemble the 1988 Wienermobile, and here it doesn't quite succeed. Instead of buns, the sausage looks like it's resting on a piece of French toast.

Before Oscar Mayer started mass-producing the updated whistles, Tom asked the engineering company if they wanted a patent on the design. The company declined. So Tom ended up with his name on the patent for the new whistles, which started appearing in 1989. The whistles even had the familiar yellow band, a sticker that Oscar Mayer paid unskilled workers a penny apiece to put on.

The Wienermobile was dramatically overhauled in 1995, and, one year later, the Wiener Whistle got a similar makeover. The 1996 whistles ditched the oversized buns in favor of a more streamlined, elegant look that perfectly mirrors the 1995 Wienermobile. It is by far the best-looking whistle Oscar Mayer has ever produced.

Back at the Walmart, I finally make it through the front door and am ready to find my teammates.

"Excuse me," says a voice to my left. I look over and see a smiling security guard. "Is that your Wienermobile?"

I don't even bother answering. "Let me go get you a whistle."

Team California gets along very well. We laugh, we cry, we ridicule each other mercilessly. But when it counts, we pull together. Like today, for example, when we worked a Bakersfield Blaze game. To make up for a previous Wienermobile cancellation, we handed out free Beanie Wienies to the first five hundred ticket holders. If you think whistles attract attention, you should see the response to a plush replica of the Wienermobile. The result was pandemonium. The crowd surged toward us, our table got tipped over, and poor Ali nearly twisted an ankle.

But no matter how well a team gets along, there's one dispute that's always threatening: where to eat. Meals can tear a team apart. Our team's meal difficulties are based on personality. Brad is a vegetarian and Sofia is ridiculously health-conscious. She works out once, sometimes twice, a day and refuses to consume anything that might taste good or contain calories. She's even scolded me for taking an after-dinner mint. "Your body doesn't know what to do with that!" she lectured.

Tonight is typical of our troubles with food. Even before our event ended at six, there was talk of dinner.

"Where does everyone want to eat?" asked Brad.

"I don't care," said Ali.

"I don't care," said Sofia.

"I don't care," said Dave.

Of course everyone cares, but no one is willing to risk an opinion. It's group dynamics 101.

After packing up at the grocery store, Brad drives us through the unfamiliar streets of Bakersfield (land of strip malls and vacant lots) in search of food. We go down a boulevard of neon signs, each promising some comfort and quick sustenance.

"There's Burger King. We could always go there," I offer.

"That sounds good," says Ali.

"We are *not* going to Burger King," says Sofia, quickly killing that idea.

Another few miles, another hundred options. "Subway?" I suggest.

"Subway's fine," says Ali.

"I'm kinda sick of Subway," says Brad.

"Yeah, me, too," adds Sofia. And so the search continues.

Thirty minutes pass. In the back of the Wienermobile, Ali and I are in visible pain. Every one of our ideas has been shot down by the health twins up front. Neanderthals had an easier time finding food.

I get really cranky when my blood sugar drops. "Can we please just pick a place?!"

"Hey, I'm trying. Do you have any suggestions?" says Brad.

"I've had, like, fifty suggestions! You guys shot them all down," I say.

"I just won't eat. I don't care. Go wherever you want," says Sofia. I'm surprised it took so long for someone to play the passive-aggressive card.

"No, we'll find someplace," says Brad.

Another thirty minutes pass. My stomach is now eating itself and Ali is slumped against the window, possibly dead. We've both given up pointing out the myriad fast food restaurants that line the boulevard. Brad is in the driver's seat, both literally and figuratively.

Just as I'm about to eat my fingernails, Brad spots a simple sign that reads VEGAN CUISINE. "How about that place?" he says.

"Oh, that looks good," says Sofia.

"Fine!" Ali and I scream back.

I've never had a vegan meal, so I already hate it. I spend dinner pouting like a sullen child as mushy, unfamiliar dishes are placed in front of me. Fortunately, no one else is in the mood for conversation. We eat silently and don't say a word on the drive back to the hotel.

Only twenty-four hours until we have to pick another place for dinner.

It's hard to run, and even harder to hide, when you're in a Wienermobile.

It's a lazy drive day as I steer us down yet another hot dog highway. As usual, Ali's in the passenger seat while Brad and Sofia hang out in the back. I hear giggling but have no idea what's going on back here. Frankly, I don't want to know.

Suddenly, flashing lights appear in the rearview mirror. "Oh my god, it's the police. We're getting pulled over," I say. My teammates fall silent.

My heart races and cool sweat starts dripping from my forehead as I slowly pull over. I watch the officer get out of his car. He takes slow, deliberate steps toward my window, pausing often to study the large fish he just landed. It takes him a while to reach my window.

"Hello, officer," I nervously squeak.

The officer makes a show out of removing his silver sunglasses. The ritual takes an eternity. Eyes free, he stares up at me. I find myself out of words.

He doesn't know what to say either. So he just starts laughing.

"Don't worry," he says in between chuckles. "You didn't do anything wrong. I just wanted to tell the guys back at the station that I pulled over the Wienermobile! Hey, you mind if I get a picture?"

The officer snaps a photo and we give him some whistles. He then heads back to his squad car, leaving me to collapse on the steering wheel.

"Man, you gotta relax," says Brad as he puts his headphones back on.

CHAPTER 13

n the 1930s, Oscar Mayer did something that no other meat company had thought to do before—appeal to children.

"That was probably their most brilliant marketing idea, to get kids," says historian Bruce Kraig. "They invented the kids' hot dog category. That's why people know the name, know the Wienermobile—it's from their childhood. Oscar Mayer realized that if you hook kids, you've got them forever."

The focus on families came from the fact that Oscar Mayer was still a close-knit family company at the time. This corporate culture allowed the freedom to create unique and innovative advertisements. And nowhere is that freedom more apparent than in the company's most famous advertisement—the Wienermobile. "When you look at the Oscar Mayer Wienermobile, it comes straight out of that family tradition," says Kraig. "It's not invented by Don Draper."

As communications executive David Armano writes in an online blog for Advertising Age, "Had Carl G. Mayer put his concept in front of a bunch of marketing executives, I'm not certain it would have ever gotten the green light to move forward. Think about it—if you never saw the Wienermobile in action, how would you estimate return on investment? How do you measure smiles? What do those get you?"

Carl G. Mayer (sometimes spelled "Karl") was responsible for dreaming up the Wienermobile. The nephew of company founder Oscar G., Carl joined the company in 1925 after graduating from the University of Wisconsin. Within a few years, he became Oscar Mayer's advertising manager.

Carl and his coworkers had some interesting ideas about how to market the Oscar Mayer brand. In the 1920s, the company used "wiener wagons" that carted around a German band. In the 1930s, there was Little Oscar, a little person dressed in a white butcher's coat and wearing a tall chef's hat who would talk up the wonders of Oscar Mayer meat. (More on him later.)

The Wienermobile evolved from earlier attempts at mobile marketing. In 1898, Montgomery Ward built two electric vehicles to use as rolling advertisements. In 1918, Pep-O-Mint Lifesavers pioneered product mobiles. "It was followed by cars shaped like Electrolux vacuum cleaners, Heinz pickles and a huge can of V-8 juice with celery sprigs emblazoned on the seats."

The Wienermobile's hot dog shape was also an evolution. "In the 1920s, there was a fad in restaurants to make the restaurant into the shape of what you're selling," says Kraig. "Why not make it mobile?"

Before landing on a mobile hot dog, Carl Mayer rejected ideas for a Wienercopter and a Wienerscooter. Instead, he decided on a more advanced version of the company's familiar wiener wagons. The first Wienermobile debuted on July 18, 1936. It was built on a Dodge chassis by General Body Company of Chicago at a cost of $5,000.

The original Wienermobile looked nothing like today's models. It was thirteen feet long and made of metal. "The wiener of the original Wienermobile was not nestled in a bun, but sat naked on a platform which had half-moon-shaped fenders on the four corners. Headlight mounts and radiator were tucked into a slit that had been created in the front of the dog." An open-cockpit design placed the totally exposed driver in the middle of the sausage. A rear cockpit was reserved for Little Oscar.

It was a plain hot dog—all red except for the familiar yellow band that advertised "U.S. Government Inspected Oscar Mayer's German wieners." "Look For The Yellow Band" was painted on the vehicle's yellow chassis.

The Wienermobile was the perfect embodiment of Oscar Mayer's family-friendly ideals and became an instant hit. According to The Big Book of Car Culture, *"Sales soared in the Chicago area almost as soon as the mobile wiener took to the streets."*

An advertising icon was born.

CHAPTER 14

This weekend we're booked at the Santa Barbara County Fair. After spending the previous five days in bleak Bakersfield, California (the strip mall capital of America), the change in scenery is dramatic and mood lifting.

We're even happier when we get to our hotel. "This is where we're staying?" I say in disbelief as we pull into the parking lot.

Somehow Sofia managed to wrangle rooms at a beautiful hotel that's just a few blocks from the ocean. For $60 a night, we get the ocean, a pool, *and* a TV in the bathroom. My suite even has two beds! It's a testament to both Sofia's negotiating skills and the Wienermobile's barter value.

Everyone was shocked when Russ first mentioned our lodging budget. We figured that $60 would get you either a crack den or an abandoned barn. But, like true adults, we've adapted and are actually living quite well on the road.

The trick is to call the hotel, ask for the sales manager, and tell them you're bringing the Oscar Mayer Wienermobile. If there's any hesitation, promise T-shirts, whistles, and Beanie Wienies. Mention all the attention the hotel will receive. It works almost every time. Not that I've tried— hotel booking is left to Sofia and Ali. In return, Brad and I load the luggage and organize the supplies. If Sofia and Ali are the brains of this operation, Brad and I are content being the brawn.

Santa Barbara is probably the most beautiful place we've visited so far. Dramatically perched next to the Pacific, the city is a series of wonders. Yesterday was an off day and the team voted to go to the beach. I deflected, not wanting to expose my pasty, flabby flesh to the harsh sun (or to Sofia).

"I think I'm just going downtown," I said.

"Okay, have fun," said Sofia.

"We'll miss you, Monkey," said Ali, using the nickname she gave me after suggesting that I look a lot like Curious George.

I had hoped that at least one of the girls, preferably Sofia, would protest my absence, but no one seems to care much. But solitude is a rare thing on the road, so I decided to treasure this unexpected alone time.

Downtown Santa Barbara is well worth a visit if you're ever in the area. Besides the countless shops and Mexican restaurants, I'd highly recommend the 1929 courthouse complex, comprising four Spanish-style buildings on a full city block in the center of town. The view alone is worth the free admission.

After a full day of sightseeing and a restful night's sleep in our luxurious surroundings, I wake rested and ready to shill for Oscar Mayer. Unfortunately, the rest of the team is a bit slower. We're supposed to meet in the lobby at seven. Knowing that my teammates hate being on time, I purposely show up at 7:05 and am still the first one in the lobby. Everyone else turns up fifteen minutes later.

Immediately I become what Ali likes to call "Moody Dave"—a sour ball of negative energy. I'll snap out of it eventually, but at the moment I want nothing to do with my tardy teammates. That'll teach 'em for being late.

Despite the delayed start, we're still among the first people to arrive at the expansive Santa Barbara fairgrounds. Dew clings to the midway and the only sounds are push brooms and the occasional clang of an errant wrench. Fairgrounds are miraculous in the morning, so calm and expansive. It's a shame they have to let people in.

Brad rides shotbun as I navigate the fairground's narrow, asphalt paths. We pass carnival workers who scurry about like ants, setting up their tents, kiosks, booths, stands, and rides. No one pays us any attention.

The carnies are an interesting subculture—a friendly, nomadic people who travel in packs. After just a few fairs, I'm surprised by the number of familiar faces. But if you own a merry-go-round, I suppose there isn't much to do except follow the fair circuit.

Carnies are a vastly understudied group. For example, I had no idea there were carny families who travel the summer circuit together. Mom and Dad set up the inflatable laser tag game while Sister and Brother wrangle business and take tickets. And when Sister and Brother get bored, they come over and bother the nice Hotdoggers.

Another interesting thing about fair life is carny currency, which is based strictly on trading. You give me a turkey leg and I'll give you a hand-woven dream catcher, that kind of thing. This has been an amazing discovery for us since we have a lot of Wienermobile swag to barter with. Last week, I swapped two Beanie Wienies for a palm reading. The fortune teller said that true love is just around the corner.

The Santa Barbara fair positions us across from a cotton candy booth and next to the inflatable laser tag center. A fan hums, delivering life-giving air to the plastic castle.

Except for running off the laser tag kids, the morning is slow and lazy. Ali and Brad leave to see if they can trade whistles for food. Sofia bolts a short time later to book more hotels. I stay behind since, well, someone has to.

By now, Share the Smiles has become second nature, which means that it only takes half your brain to do a convincing job. So while the work can be dull, the human psychology of it is endlessly fascinating.

Already, I'm amazed by how many people confuse the Wienermobile with a confessional or a psychiatrist's office.

Today, one man told Sofia and Brad about how his brother had a whistle when they were young and he was blowing on it when he fell down and knocked his tooth out. So the man wanted to send his brother a new one for his birthday. And there was the man who wanted a whistle for the boy he took out of an abusive relationship. "He calls me Dad," said the beaming gentleman.

The elderly especially enjoy baring their souls. They've spent a lifetime accumulating stories and now no one wants to listen. The grandkids don't answer the phone and their friends are deaf, so it must be a relief to find such a captive audience.

A stooped, graying woman came up to the table today, laughing and giggling about the Wienermobile. We asked if she wanted a picture and she said she wanted to grab her husband first. "He might want one," she said. "He's an old-timer, and he might not be around next year, so I should get a picture to remember him by."

She came back later, dragging her husband toward the Wienermobile. The funny thing was that while the man wasn't happy about having his picture taken (this was obviously a favor), he seemed to be in excellent health.

The next confession comes from a real clown. No, really, he's a clown named Poppo . . . with big shoes and oversized pants. Poppo was sent over by the food bank to help us raise money. At first I was offended. "We don't need some clown telling us how to raise money!" But Poppo quickly wins me over with two balloon animal puppies.

Poppo's real name is Bob, but he won't answer to that while in uniform. The man's dedicated, but he's also not your average clown. Poppo is neither spry nor particularly energetic. Patches of gray peek out from an exaggerated funnel hat, and his movements are slow, often cautious. His balloon animal style isn't flashy, but his repertoire—dogs, snakes, snails, rabbits—is solid.

Despite my initial misgivings, Poppo's presence greatly boosts our donations. Poppo proves so popular that most of the kids don't even notice the giant hot dog behind them; all they see is the sweet promise of twisted latex.

After a few hours of work, Poppo looks beat. "Would you mind if I sat in the hot dog for a few minutes?" he asks. "My feet are killing me."

I agree to accompany Poppo and hand off my Wienermobile supply apron (yes, we wear aprons) to Sofia. I'm thankful for a break, as well. We step inside and each plop down in a relish-colored captain's chair.

"So, how did you get started with this?" I ask.

"My son was a single dad. And five years ago, he died suddenly. So I took my grandkids home and raised them. You know, like they were my own. I wanted something that would keep 'em busy, so I decided to enroll them in a clown troupe. Eventually I joined, too—group called the Kadiddlehoppers, a small-time outfit made up of some local Elks members. A few years later I was elected grand jester."

Poppo pauses, savoring the memory. "At my coronation dinner, they served wine and prime rib."

Poppo goes on to explain that the Kadiddlehoppers perform at parades, visit hospitals and nursing homes, and do other charity work. Their entire operating budget comes from a raffle held at the beginning of the year. Time and talent are all volunteered.

"Well, the kids here seem to love it," I say. "You're way more popular than we are."

Poppo brushes aside the flattery and looks out the window at the busy merry-go-round spinning behind us. "Every child is amazing," he says.

Poppo then unfastens a round Kadiddlehopper pin from his rainbow suspenders and hands it to me. "Come on, kid. Break time's over."

CHAPTER 15

By this point in our tenure, no one enjoys driving the Wienermobile. The job's still a thrill, but the vehicle is so unbelievably uncomfortable that even sitting shotbun is a chore. The most coveted spots are in the way back, where, with some clever rearranging of luggage, you can fashion a makeshift bed. Lying down makes the trip somewhat less like vacationing in hell.

It would be nice if driving chores were split evenly, but that's seldom the case. Usually, the men bear the brunt of the miles. It's not that Ali and Sofia are slacking, just that Brad and I feel it's our manly duty to stay behind the wheel. The things guys will do to prove their machismo.

I sometimes think Brad derives some sick pleasure out of a marathon drive. He'll rest his boombox on the engine cover, plug in his headphones, and drift off into his own world.

My driving philosophy is to stop as little as possible. Pulling off so my partners can go to the bathroom? *No. Let's just get twenty more miles.* If we stop, we're going to be delayed for so long. So my plan is minimal stops. Do not drink anything. Let's just get there.

Very little is off limits when you spend so much time crammed together with people. Even the topics I'd rather not cover, like menstruation and the mysteries of the female orgasm, eventually come up. Of these things I'm completely naïve.

Sofia tends to be more modest around delicate conversation, but Ali has no problem being bold. We've heard how she lost her virginity a few times already.

Like Sofia, I do my best to remain silent when the talk turns blue. It's not out of any Puritan beliefs; it's just that my sex life is completely uninteresting. I've had sex, sure, but almost exclusively under the influence of alcohol, making the details harder to remember.

But unless you crawl under the luggage pile, there's no place to hide in the Wienermobile. Eventually I fall under the hot lights. "So, Dave, how did you lose your virginity?" asks Ali during a particularly tedious drive.

"I really don't—"

"Oh come on," she says. "Stop being such a prude."

"Fine," I say, summoning all my storytelling courage. "It actually happened in Scotland."

"Scotland?" says Brad. It's hard to get his attention, but now he seems interested.

"Yeah, a bunch of us went there for spring break."

"When?" asks Sofia.

"Oh, last year," I lie. The deed actually happened just a few months ago, but I can't let my peers know I was such a late bloomer. It's important to maintain the appearance of being a stud, especially in front of Sofia.

"So we were in Edinburgh and my buddy Kit and I went to this night club called Subway where we met these two girls, Kat and Jodi. So I start talking to Jodi and Kit starts talking to Kat."

"Kit started talking to Kat?" says Ali. "That's hilarious."

"Yeah, they made a cute couple. Anyway, I'm talking to Jodi and we hit it off. We were dancing and having a good time. And at one point, I look over to see Kat sitting on the floor, slumped against the wall while

Kit is kneeling next to her singing 'Brown Eyed Girl.' Jodi and I decide to leave and I walk her back to her place, this nice two-story apartment building somewhere in Edinburgh. So we're standing there and she asks if I want to come upstairs."

"Oooooh," says Sofia, clearly enjoying my embarrassment.

"We go upstairs and she pulls me into her room and we start making out on the bed. Things are really heating up, we're both totally naked, and I'm thinking, 'This is it! It's finally gonna happen!' And then she leans in and whispers, 'Do you have a condom?'

"And I say, 'No. Don't you have one?' And she says, 'No.' I ask if her roommates have any condoms. She says they don't. Then she says, 'I'm not gonna do anything without a condom.' So now I'm starting to get panicked. Here I've got this naked girl lying in front of me, ready to go, and suddenly we're not gonna have sex."

"What did you do?" asks Ali.

"I asked her where the nearest drugstore was."

Sofia gasps. "You didn't."

"I did. I asked where the nearest drugstore was and she said it was right down the street.

"'Stay right here,' I told her as I put on my pants. Then I ran down the stairs and I'm sprinting through the streets of Edinburgh, looking for this drugstore. And eventually I find it, right around the corner. So I run into this store, totally out of breath, and I tell the cashier, 'Hey, I need some condoms.' And this guy, who's totally confused about the out-of-breath American who just wandered into his shop, slowly hands me a box of condoms. I throw down some money and run back down to her apartment."

"She was still there, I hope," says Brad.

"She was, but she was sleeping."

"Oh my god," says Ali.

"So I had to wake her up and show her the box of condoms."

"Davey!" shrieks Sofia.

"And that's how it happened."

"Wow," says Brad. "Wow."

The team all cracks up. It's a good story, although not terribly romantic.

Being on the road hasn't helped my sex life like I thought it would. Things with Sofia are at a frustrating standstill, and it's tough to meet postpubescent girls when you spend your days stationed next to the Tilt-a-Whirl.

The only thing keeping me going is an intense e-mail flirtation with Margot, a Mizzou grad I met my last night on campus. Margot is a sprite, barely over five feet tall, and the very definition of adorable. Unfortunately, she lives in Kansas City and I have no fixed address. But we exchanged info before I left and, despite distance and different time zones, have done an admirable job keeping in touch.

Actually, I think things are going so well with Margot because we don't actually have to speak. Plus, with so much distance there's never any consideration of commitment. It's just about the perfect relationship.

Yet, still I hold a tiny torch for my partner. "So, Sofia," I say with a sly smile, "Tell us about your first time."

"You wish," she says and goes right back to reading her magazine.

"I could tell my story again," says Ali.

CHAPTER 16

There's something strange going on with Brad and Sofia. At events, they're pretty much inseparable. They go on break together, they refill supplies together, they count the donation money together. It's an awful lot of togetherness. *Too much* togetherness, if you ask me.

What happened to the grand romance between Sofia and me? It lived in my head for a few weeks, but has failed to make the leap into reality. There's just no driving a wedge between her and Brad. I've tried to get her alone, tried to charm her, tried to be funny—nothing's worked. Sofia and I are stuck in a friendship. Which rarely leads to sex.

Ali and I have our suspicions about exactly what's going on between Brad and Sofia. They seem more buddy-buddy than most buddies, but we haven't witnessed anything unprofessional. If they're hiding something, they're hiding it very well.

We're on another marathon trek over the engine-cranking Tehachapi Mountains. Brad drives, lazily swaying to the Bill Withers soul classic "Ain't No Sunshine." This is one of the few tapes we own, so each song is bolted to our brains. Sofia sits next to him, furiously scribbling in her diary. In the back, basking in a generous amount of reflected engine heat, are Ali and me. She's reading a magazine; I'm flipping through a *USA Today* I swiped from the front desk. I love hotels that offer free newspapers. It's what gets me up in the morning.

It's shaping up to be another long, boring drive when suddenly a most unexpected thing happens—Sofia casually puts her diary down on the engine cover.

"THERE'S AN OPEN DIARY ON THE ENGINE COVER!" I want to scream. How am I the only one noticing this?

Maybe it's just that I'm nosier than most. But, hey, teammates shouldn't have secrets. If we're going to make this trip work, we all need to be completely open and honest with each other. Okay, I know it's wrong to look at another person's diary. But I also know that I'm still going to do it.

I lean in as casually as possible. The words are tiny, cursive blurs that I can barely make out. I lean closer, still shocked that such good fortune hasn't been ruined yet. Eyes squinting hard, I quickly decipher a sentence at the top of the page: *Last night, Brad and I kissed.*

WHAT?!!

This is bigger news than anything in *USA Today*. This may be the biggest news in Hotdogger history—verifiable proof that Brad and Sofia have been having a secret relationship. How could I have been so blind?! Suddenly, all those shared lunches and joint trips to refill the whistle bag make sense. You don't need two people to refill the whistle bag. Hell, you barely need *one* person to do it.

Ain't no sunshine when she's gone.

The news is too much to keep to myself so I covertly poke Ali's leg.

"What?" she says, clearly annoyed.

I lean in so close that I'm practically in her ear. "Sofia kissed Brad," I whisper.

It's not warm when she's away.

"What?! How do you know?"

I point to the diary that's still open on the engine cover. "Her diary."

"You read her diary?" she whispers. "You can't do that!"

Ain't no sunshine when she's gone.

"She just left it there. But, come on, Brad and Sofia are dating!"

It takes a moment for the news to fully register with Ali. "Wow."

And she's always gone too long anytime she goes away.

Sofia and Brad are an item. Life on the road will never be the same.

Russ once told us, "There are no secrets. You can't hide in a Wiener-mobile." I remember this pearl of wisdom as I contemplate the Brad/Sofia situation. Ali and I know that Brad and Sofia are dating. Brad and Sofia know they're dating. The real question is—do Brad and Sofia know we know they're dating? If so, they haven't said anything. And we certainly haven't said anything. It's a lot of silence about a topic that affects all of us.

I have no clue how long this relationship's been going on, but I suspect it started sometime around Hot Dog High. Right about the time I fell for her.

Alas, our romance was unrequited, unexpressed, and unrealistic. Way too many "uns" for anything to happen. To be honest, I never expected to get the girl. I never expect to get any girl. Girls go for confident cowboys with good skin like Brad. Or John Wayne.

Sofia and Brad dating has altered team dynamics a bit, even if they're not "out in the open" about their relationship. Now, we're two teams. The lovebirds spent a lot of their free time together, under the guise of "doing laundry" or "grabbing dinner," leaving Ali and I to entertain each other.

"So, what do you want to do tonight?" Ali asks me after a day at the fair.

"What are Brad and Sofia doing?"

"Laundry."

"Sure they are," I say.

"We could go see a movie."

"I guess," responding with nothing resembling enthusiasm.

Ali and I spend a quiet evening watching Stanley Kubrick's *Eyes Wide Shut*. It's a good thing we aren't on a date because *Eyes Wide Shut* would've ruined it—it's not a very romantic film. We're walking back to the hotel when Ali spots something.

"Hey, it's Brad and Sofia."

I immediately see the secret couple across the street. They're holding hands and laughing. It's enough to make you sick.

"Should we follow them?" I ask.

Ali gives me a puzzled look. "Why would we follow them?"

"I don't know. To see what they're doing."

"You really want to know?"

"Good point."

So Ali and I go one way, Sofia and Brad go the other, two couples who couldn't be more different.

CHAPTER 17

Quincy, California, is beautiful. It's also boring as hell.

Located in northeastern California, Quincy has fewer than two thousand residents, most of whom are white. It's the only town in Plumas County to have a chain grocery store, and residents recently celebrated the arrival of a Subway sandwich shop. While the community is small, the space is picturesque. Quincy is nestled in the northern Sierra Nevada, safe in a green valley encircled by thick forest.

We're staying at a small motel on the northern outskirts of town. It's a two-story, L-shaped complex with a dusty parking lot and a sassy receptionist.

"We should have four rooms," says Sofia when checking in.

The receptionist, long blonde hair falling upon a wrinkled denim vest, looks up the reservation on a sheet of yellowed notebook paper. "Yup, got you down for four rooms. I got three nonsmoking and one smoking."

Sofia's ears immediately perk up. "That should be four nonsmoking rooms. I reserved four nonsmoking rooms." When something isn't 100 percent right, Sofia will let you know it.

"Sorry, only got three. Fair's in town, you know."

"Yeah, we know," says Sofia in a "don't mess with me" tone.

Normally, sorting out who gets the smoking room would take hours and countless rounds of rock-paper-scissors. But today Brad steps up and volunteers to take the room. *I hope he chokes on all that smoke,* I think.

It's not that I dislike Brad. I'm just jealous of him. The man won Sofia. And now I'm alone in the most depressing hotel room I've ever seen—one window, scant lighting, and all wood paneling. It's like a rustic prison.

My only companion for the night is a thirteen-inch TV that gets five channels, three of them nothing but static. I soon give up on that idea and try to think of some other form of amusement. I could read, but the light's so dim that I'd probably go blind. So the only thing to do is go to bed. At ten o'clock.

My first night in Quincy is truly a dark night of the soul. Lying in bed, my eyes affixed to the water-stained ceiling, I shuffle through every mistake I've ever made. An abbreviated list:

* Taking Beth Connley to homecoming
* Being too sarcastic
* Being too moody in the morning
* Never finding love
* Not getting more involved at college
* Often wearing jeans that are too short

Morning takes forever to arrive. We all meet in the parking lot at 8 a.m., and I'm heartened to find my partners similarly bleary-eyed.

"This place sucks," I say bitterly to Sofia.

"Hey, you try finding a hotel room in Quincy." She's got a point.

At least the fair is lively. The Wienermobile is parked next to a small stage that hosts a variety of carny entertainment. There are the Amazing Harmonatra Brothers ("a couple of Irish boys traveling the country singing traditional American music") and Rex's Broken Top lumberjack show.

Rex seems like a real lumberjack, complete with a flannel shirt carefully torn to highlight his elm-like arms and a ridiculously large axe. The great thing about Rex's thirty-minute show is that it includes twenty-five minutes of lumberjack banter and tree jokes and about five minutes of actual tree-chopping. But those five minutes are riveting.

When in strange towns, it's important to sample the local cuisine. During a morning break, Brad and I take the rental car into town for some breakfast. I'm willing to put our differences (or *my* differences) aside for some food. One circle around downtown (which takes about three minutes) and we settle on the Morning Thunder Café. This must be the popular destination since even on fair day we have to wait for a table.

But the wait is well worth it. I consider myself an omelet connoisseur, and never have I had a better one than at the Morning Thunder. Huge, fluffy, and overstuffed with fresh veggies, this is the reason God invented the egg. I'm so glad we didn't stop by the gas station and pick up a box of donuts, as was my first suggestion.

Brad and I take our time eating, but eventually must return to work. We arrive back at the fair with breathless news of the greatest breakfast ever made.

"You have to try the Morning Thunder Café. It's amazing," I tell the girls.

"Amazing," agrees Brad.

Never one to miss a good meal, Ali immediately grabs her purse. "Come on, Sofia, let's go."

The girls rush off, leaving Brad and I alone with the lumberjack show. An hour later, our partners return. "How was breakfast?" I ask.

"They were closed," says a crestfallen Ali.

"Closed? We were just there."

"Yeah, they close at noon. Thanks," says Ali.

Brad and I sense an easy kill. "That's too bad, because you missed the best breakfast ever," he says.

"The omelet was unbelievable. I doubt I'll ever have a better one," I say.

"Oh, no way you'll ever find a better one," agrees Brad.

Stone-faced, Ali drops her purse and hastily refastens her work apron. "I hate you both."

There are many mysteries on the road. What's the difference between freeways and highways? Why is the hotel minibar so expensive? What's that stain on my bedspread? But there's one riddle that baffles me the most: Why don't chicks dig the Wienermobile?

Like ketchup and peanut butter, love and the Wienermobile do not mix (Sofia and Brad excluded, of course). In fact, this car seems to repel more women than it attracts. It's strange, I know. When I took the job, I figured that the Wienermobile would provide me with the single greatest opening line in history. Something like, "Would you care to step outside and see my twenty-seven-foot-long wiener?"

But that—and every other hot dog–related icebreaker—has failed miserably. Try explaining the job to an attractive lady and you're met with either a confused stare or an awkward laugh. Not that you get to meet many attractive women at grocery stores and county fairs. Sad to say, but as far as sexually attractive professions go, Hotdogger is right below trout gutter.

Personally, I feel lied to. During Hot Dog High, there were whispers of a Wienermobile Club. I figured we were all in it, but it turns out this is a more illicit group, made up of people who have had sex in the Wienermobile. Who cares if the club actually exists, I want to join.

Right now, membership seems impossible. It's difficult enough to find willing women. Take that group and subdivide by girls who enjoy straddling a carpeted engine cover. You're now looking at a very small sample. It's like finding a slutty needle in the world's largest haystack.

But there is some hope because Margot, my e-mail buddy from Mizzou, is visiting this week. Our notes have gotten increasingly flirtatious, but I was still shocked when she mentioned coming to meet me in San Diego.

"You really want to fly out?" I asked. "You know we're traveling in a giant hot dog, right?"

"I know," she said in her high, always energetic voice. "I just think it would be so cool to see the Wienermobile! And you, of course."

Maybe Margot only likes me for my hot dog. It doesn't matter. Just the thought of joining the exclusive Wienermobile Club is enough to jump at the visit. Plus, this is going to make Sofia totally jealous.

Margot flew in a few days ago and was as adorable as ever. She may not weigh more than ninety pounds, but her cuteness is gigantic. She has porcelain skin, short black hair, and wide green eyes. She almost looks like a doll—but one you want to take home and do unspeakable things with.

We got off to a good start. There's no better way to make an impression than picking someone up from the airport in a Wienermobile. Immediately she was a celebrity, the envy of all incoming passengers. "This is so cool!" she shrieked.

While Sofia was fairly indifferent to Margot's visit, Ali hasn't been overly enthusiastic.

"So, what do you think?" I asked her after the airport.

"She seems nice," said Ali.

"Seems nice?"

"I don't know. She's tiny."

"So?"

"Well, she just seems a little mousy."

"Mousy? What does that mean?"

"You know—tiny, cute, doesn't say much. You know, like a mouse."

"A mouse doesn't giggle."

"You like mousy girls. There's nothing wrong with it. That's just your type."

"It's not my type. I didn't even know mousy was a category until two minutes ago."

"Oh, you knew."

I have no idea what Ali's talking about. Margot's not mousy. Although she does have a cute giggle.

The first night with Margot was a bit awkward. We had never hugged for longer than five seconds, let alone kissed. So we just laid in the dark for a long while and talked. Eventually we ran out of things to say and a thick silence moved in. That's when kissing seemed like a good idea.

The second night was much the same, although with less talking and more kissing.

The third day, she came along on a Wienermobile store visit. "I can't believe you guys do this for a job!" she said while joyfully passing out whistles. I could practically hear Ali raise her eyebrows.

Fortunately, Margot and I are free from my teammates tonight. And to seal the deal, I've romantically stocked the mini fridge with alcohol.

I'm three beers in before she even finishes her first drink. "So . . . what do you want to do tonight?" I ask, trying to suppress my slur. It's a loaded question. We both know what she wants to do.

"I don't know. What do you want to do?"

"I don't know."

The mating dance has begun.

I stare at Margot and she stares back. She takes a sip from her bottle and I take one from mine. I laugh nervously and she continues to stare.

Perhaps fearing that this could go on forever, Margot thankfully makes the first move. She rests her Zima on the nightstand and leans in for a kiss. Our lips meet and I taste the sweet tang of lemony alcohol on her lips.

"That was nice," she purrs.

Margot smiles a devilish grin I didn't even know she was capable of. This is no mouse; this is a woman. Margot wrestles the beer bottle from my vice-like grip and puts it on the nightstand. She then dives in, confidently pushing me against the mattress. This *is* very nice.

Our make-out session is going well, perhaps a bit too well. My window to join the Wienermobile Club is about to slam shut.

I come up for air, breaking the lip lock. "You know . . . we should . . . we should go down to the Wienermobile."

Margot laughs, but doesn't slow down. She continues to lavish affection on my lips, cheek, and neck. I want to enjoy the moment, but my mind keeps drifting back to the Club. This might be my only chance to join, I have to try again.

"It could be funny."

"What could be funny?" Margot says in between gentle, fragrant kisses.

"You know, the Wienermobile. Going down to the Wienermobile."

"Why do you want to go to the Wienermobile?"

There are times to answer a woman's questions honestly. This is not one of those times. What am I supposed to say? *Margot, I want to have sex in the Wienermobile so I can brag about it at the next Hot Dog High.* A lie is definitely called for in this case.

"What? You've never wanted to roll around in a giant hot dog?" I say in my most seductive tone.

"Um . . . no," she says. "I'm happy right here."

"I just don't want you to regret it later."

"I'll be okay." Margot starts in again with the kisses, her lips zigzagging across my face.

Yeah, I'm fine with this too. This is totally cool. Really, I'm completely happy with absolutely everything.

"I just think—"

Margot stops. Cold. She pulls back, props herself up on my chest, and gives me a long stare. "Dave, we are not going to the Wienermobile."

It's never fun to get reprimanded, especially when you're heading for second base. Quickly, I try to improvise a way out of this mess. "Kidding! Just kidding!" Without giving her time to fixate on my curious fetish, I pull Margot close and continue the make-out session. Thank god she's so forgiving.

Hmmm. I wonder if she'd be up for doing it in the rental car?

CHAPTER 18

You can't examine the early history of the Wienermobile without mentioning the man it was designed for, Little Oscar, the world's smallest chef. Right before he created the Wienermobile, advertising manager Carl Mayer came up with Little Oscar. Quite a productive few months at the office.

The idea most likely evolved from performers that Carl hired to entertain customers on Oscar Mayer's early wiener wagons. But historian Bruce Kraig suggests that the roots of Little Oscar can be traced back even further, to German folklore that was heavy on tales of dwarves and gnomes. "That's very German," says Kraig. "And I asked Oscar G. if that was where Little Oscar came from and he said, 'Yeah, that's possible. There were a lot of Germans around and we were raised on those stories.'"

Little Oscar proved to be a big hit with Chicagoland customers, and Carl Mayer began brainstorming ways to use his latest creation. "We felt we had to have something very special for Little Oscar to get around in," said Carl. "The Wienermobile was the answer."

The first Little Oscar was a little person named Meinhardt Raabe (pronounced "Robby"). After graduating from the University of Wisconsin, Raabe couldn't find work. He recalled being told, "You don't belong here.

You belong in a carnival." But Raabe persevered and was eventually hired by Oscar Mayer in 1936 to be Little Oscar. He would visit stores, pass out samples, and entertain customers.

He also got to travel in the very first Wienermobile. "Raabe rode out in the open in a sort of rumble seat high up in the back end of the thirteen-foot wiener. To assume his perch, he had to be hoisted into place. At first the driver too was in an open cockpit. Later, a boxy glass enclosure was added for the driver's—though not Little Oscar's—comfort."

According to Raabe, the 1936 Wienermobile was not a luxurious ride. "It wasn't like a sedan by any means." Raabe also recalls the difficulties he and the driver had when they took the Wienermobile on the road. "We would stay at motels at night. Some of the motels thought it was a truck and would not be appropriate. So we went to another place down the road where they appreciated having the Wienermobile as an attraction."

In 1938, Raabe left Oscar Mayer for the promise of Hollywood. He was cast in The Wizard of Oz, playing the Munchkin City coroner who proclaimed that the Wicked Witch was "most sincerely dead."

Raabe returned to Oscar Mayer after filming ended. Asked how he felt about originating the role of Little Oscar, Raabe was characteristically humble. "Let's face it—it was better than having to dig ditches." Meinhardt Raabe died in 2010 at the age of ninety-four.

Besides being the first Little Oscar, Raabe also recruited George Molchan, the man who would become most closely associated with the role. Raabe visited Molchan's hometown of Gary, Indiana, and became a mentor to the teen. In 1951, Raabe contacted Molchan about interviewing to become one of the Little Oscars. Molchan not only got the job, he would go on to hold it for thirty-six years.

Molchan was four feet, four inches tall. "I used to say ten wieners high. You know, that's just about what it comes out to." As Little Oscar, Molchan had a variety of duties. "At the beginning of each week, he would pop out of [the Wienermobile's] hatch at smaller retailers, schools, orphanages, and children's hospitals. The end of the week was reserved for parades and promotions at larger grocery stores."

Molchan truly loved his job. He once told an interviewer, "I don't know how many times people in small towns would tell me, 'You're the biggest thing that ever hit our town.' And I'll never forget the crippled kids in hospitals, the way they'd brighten, the way those kids would sparkle."

Lilian Martin, Molchan's sister, recalled what a celebrity her brother was. "It was always a madhouse [at grocery stores]. These kids would come storming in and everybody wanted to just grab onto him. The policeman had to pick him up and put him over the fence because he would have got trampled."

Despite the occasional stampedes, Molchan enjoyed entertaining kids. "You can't outfox the children," he said. "They'd ask how old I was and I'd tell them I was seven and a half. One kid pulled my pant leg and said, 'You're not seven and a half; you got hairy legs!'"

To most people, George Molchan was Little Oscar. The company seemed to think so, as well. When Molchan retired in 1987, Oscar Mayer retired the character. When Molchan died in 2005 at the age of eighty-two, a Wienermobile led the funeral procession and mourners sang "I wish I were an Oscar Mayer wiener" while tooting on whistles.

Although Molchan was the most well-known Little Oscar, he was actually one of eight men who played the role. The small spokesmen were hired through newspaper ads, referrals from other Little Oscars, or with the help of a local little people's association.

Jerry Maren was the West Coast Little Oscar for twelve years. Maren started out as a wrestler under names like Mighty Atom, Baby Face Maren, and Tiny Terror. In The Wizard of Oz, he played the Lollipop Kid who has the honor of handing Dorothy a lollipop.

Unlike Molchan, Maren wasn't so fond of the job. "I used to get sick every weekend. Every kid was my size. I'd meet them and say, 'Hiya, pal.' And they'd breathe on me and every third one had a runny nose or cold."

While Molchan was visiting kids in the hospital, Maren seems to have struggled with a desire to put kids in the hospital. "I never hit a kid yet, but I was doing twenty-six shows in a day. People would call and say they wanted the Wienermobile and Little Oscar here, there, everywhere, so I said, 'I think I had enough.' I didn't want to turn against the children. I don't know whether it was me or them. Mostly it was them."

CHAPTER 19

On the road, even the simple stuff is difficult.

Take laundry, for example. We were given only a few Wienermobile shirts and shorts and it's a struggle to keep them clean, especially when you're working in 100-degree heat and constantly surrounded by cotton candy. We're all too cheap to drop off laundry with the hotel, so plenty of nights have been spent at the local laundromat, trying to act as surprised as everyone else that there's a Wienermobile in the parking lot.

Keeping in touch is also tough. The office gave us a rudimentary cell phone but, much like the Wienermobile, it's usually broken. With no fixed address and no permanent phone number, friends and family have to jump through a few hoops to reach you. The easiest way is via Audix, Oscar Mayer's wondrous answering service. We each have a 1-800 number and a unique extension. Call the number, dial the extension, and you can leave me a message.

Audix is highly addictive. Between the four of us, we probably check our messages several hundred times a day. Sometimes, a friend or family member will call to catch up. That always buoys the soul. However, most of the time, it's just other Hotdoggers leaving random missives. Once in awhile, Russ will send a Hotdogger-wide announcement, something like, "I would like to remind everyone that the Wienermobiles should be washed on a regular basis. Let's keep our dogs clean."

Another challenge is mail. Once a week, the office bundles up our respective mail and overnights it to wherever we're staying. Mail day is a lot like Christmas. We all fight over the bulky manila package, tearing into it like sugar-fed five-year-olds.

Today is an especially exciting mail day because the office has promised to include our new schedules. Supposedly there will be some "radical changes," and we're all looking forward to seeing where Team California is heading next. We hope it will be out of California, since we've covered every square inch of this state.

Ali, Brad, and I gather in Sofia's room to open the package. Tossing aside bills, magazines, even letters from our families, we pull out the four sheets of paper that describe our destinies.

"What?!" shrieks Ali.

"Oh my God, it's true," says Sofia. "They're really doing it."

I scan the new schedule and soon find the source of the shock. Brad and Sofia will be taking HOTDOGG'N to southern Texas border towns for a tour of Hispanic grocery stores. Ali and I will be picking up a newly retrofitted '95 Wienermobile for a two-month tour of Arizona and New Mexico.

The change is staggering. Team California is breaking up.

Ali and Sofia look ready to cry as they hug each other over and over.

"I'm going to miss you so much!" says Ali.

"I'm going to miss *you* so much!" says Sofia.

Meanwhile, Brad and I sway awkwardly in our respective corners of the room, not sure how to handle anything resembling emotion.

I understand that the office wants to keep things fresh, but it's a shame they decided to fracture such a solid team. Driving the Wienermobile is like being tossed in prison—you can't choose your cellmates and everyone becomes awfully close. I know Sofia won't sleep on a hotel comforter (too many germs). I know Brad wants to be a comedian. I know where, how, when, and to whom Ali lost her virginity. And I know way more than I should about feminine hygiene.

But at least Brad and Sofia get a Mexican honeymoon. And at least I get to escape the sappy sweetness of their constant happiness. Brad won, and I wish them well. Besides, who knows? Maybe Ali and I will fall in love somewhere just past Phoenix. Or maybe I'll settle down with someone from housekeeping.

That's the great thing about life on the road: every day there's a new turn.

I realize that Team California is officially over when I find myself in St. Louis, staring not at the blue Pacific, but at a dingy industrial park right off I-70. A few days ago, Brad and Sofia took us to the airport. It's fun to get picked up from the airport in the Wienermobile, not so fun to get dropped off in one.

"You take care, David," said Brad. "Keep an eye on Ali."

"Hey! Look! Wienermobile!"

"Bye, Monkey," said Sofia. "I'll miss you."

"Can we get some whistles?!"

We did our best to ignore the cries, cheers, whoops, and waves of our fans, but it's difficult to have an emotionally satisfying goodbye when you're standing in front of the Wienermobile.

Ali and I must now get used to being our own team. We have to decide who's going to book the hotels (Ali), who's going to plot the routes (me), and who's going to plan our off days (joint custody). Fortunately, we've already accumulated so many miles together so there shouldn't be much of an adjustment.

"Just remember that I'm in charge," I tell Ali on our first day together.

"Yeah . . . right. I'll remember that."

We're in St. Louis to pick up a retrofitted '95 Wienermobile from Craftsmen Industries, a manufacturer of custom promotional vehicles.

Retrofitting is the new buzzword around the Wienermobile department. All the '95 hot dogs are being rotated through Craftsmen for various repairs and upgrades. The old, hydraulic-operated doors are being replaced with lighter, simpler models that don't require any mechanics to open. The front glass, which was custom-shaped and difficult to replace, is being swapped for a more standard cut. And the whole vehicle is getting vacuumed.

But, as Russ often points out, nothing with the Wienermobile is ever fast or easy. We were supposed to pick up OUR DOG yesterday and drive it to northern Texas. But Craftsmen forgot to put in seat belts, a locking door, and some other minor details. Then the brakes stuck. Then the water pump broke. Then the front tires needed to be aligned. Basically, the thing is being held together by duct tape at this point.

Russ is in town supervising this important Wienermobile milestone. I must give him credit; the man is very thorough. This morning, Russ spent two hours picking apart the Wienermobile while the nervous Craftsmen manager trailed behind, taking notes. Russ wanted the camera adjusted, the headlights realigned, and the whole thing cleaned. "And I would have liked it to be on the road yesterday."

Twenty-seven hours after our scheduled departure, Ali and I climb into OUR DOG for the first time. Having just come from the dark and dismal '88, this refurbished vehicle is a revelation. It's so open, so light. If the '88 was like working in a cave, the '95 is like swimming through a rainbow. It's that bright.

Ali and I joust for the honor of getting behind the wheel first. The thrill is back; we both want to drive again. I playfully shove Ali aside and race to the driver's seat.

Poor Russ is so exhausted from a day of browbeating mechanics that he can't even manage a full wave. From the panoramic sideview mirror, I watch him nod as we pull away, a Craftsmen employee cowering by his side.

OUR DOG is a lot of fun to drive. With a new transmission and improved shocks, it's definitely a smoother ride. And unlike the '88, which shakes when you go above sixty, the '95 is built for speed. This thing can go sixty-five, no problem.

One thing is certain, there's no hiding in the '95. All the front cabin glass makes it more aquarium than automobile. As expected, Ali can't get enough of this new attention. Sitting high in the passenger's seat, she's already waving at every man, woman, car, tree, and bird we pass.

"You know you're waving at a stop sign, right?" I say after a few minutes of this ridiculousness.

"Don't tell me how to wave," she responds. And then goes right back to waving.

I'm thankful we're transitioning from the '88 to the '95 and not the other way around. What a huge letdown that would be. Kristy, who had already been on the road for a few months before we showed up, was forced to make that tragic swap. "I threw a hissy fit. I told Russ, 'You've got to be kidding me; I am not driving that damn thing! It is the ugliest Wienermobile I've ever seen. I've been driving a new one the entire time; I am not going to drive that!'" Of course, Russ made her drive it.

We're about an hour outside of St. Louis when Ali suddenly pipes up, a note of concern in her voice. "Dave, I think there's something wrong with this window," she says, gesturing to one of the back windows.

"What's wrong?"

"I think it's falling off."

Quickly, I pull over to the side of the highway, beaching us on the gravel shoulder. From the inside, the window looks a bit askew. From the outside, it looks a lot askew. The black caulk used to hold the window in place is melting, causing the large piece of glass to slowly slide out of its frame. The window hasn't moved very far yet, but I'd rather not be on the road when it finally peels off and crashes onto the interstate.

I call Russ and explain the problem.

"The window's about to *what*?"

"Fall off."

"Fall off?"

"Yes. Fall off."

Russ sighs mightily into the phone. "Better bring it back here."

OUR DOG may be an upgrade, but it's still a Wienermobile.

The Wienermobile comes home (my home, actually).

Driving on Daytona Beach, Florida.

Some sleek machines.

HOTDOGG'N takes a break in the Tehachapi Pass.

The Sound of Wiener.

German gas gawkers.

HOTDOGG'N is all smiles in California.

Punny license plate.

Filling up BIG BUN for the first time in Germany.

Trying to stay cool as the engine overheats . . . again.

Only later did we notice that Germany was 1 kilometer away.

OUR DOG makes a friend in Albuquerque.

Refurbishing a '95 Wienermobile at Craftsmen in St. Louis.

Last day on the job, U.S. Army Garrison Schinnen, the Netherlands.

Debbie trying to unlock the Wienermobile.

CHAPTER 20

aving gotten all that "getting to know you" crap out of the way, Ali and I are now like an old married couple—completely comfortable around each other and not the least bit interested in sex.

Our terrific twosome has covered a lot of ground in the past few weeks, including several days watching large people in tight cowboy shirts at the West Texas Fair and Rodeo in Abilene. If you're going to wear a cowboy shirt, make sure it fits.

Our travels have taken us all over the Southwest, a region I never before had the opportunity to visit. Ali, to her credit, is always game for adventure, and we've discovered a mutual love of national parks. So far we've taken the Wienermobile to White Sands, Carlsbad Caverns, and Bandelier National Monument in Santa Fe.

White Sands was a highlight. Located in New Mexico, it's the world's largest gypsum dune field, covering 275 miles of desert. The park's name is definitely accurate; just white sand dunes as far as the eye can see. We thought the rangers might not allow us in with the Wienermobile, but they couldn't have been happier to see us. They came out from the guard gate, took pictures, and offered to guide us around the park. Taking the eight-mile scenic drive in a Wienermobile definitely turned a few heads, the orange and yellow paint job providing a striking contrast against the white sand.

The real beauty of driving across America is that there's so much unexpected to see. The perfect example was our brief stop in Cloudcroft, New Mexico. The city is just a blip on the map, so unknown that Fodor's named Cloudcroft the number three "Most Overlooked and Underrated Destination Spot" in 2002.

I don't know what the top two choices were, but Cloudcroft was robbed. Located nineteen miles from White Sands and 8,600 feet above sea level, Cloudcroft is a quiet village of fewer than eight hundred residents. The name fits, as Cloudcroft seems to have been built upon a foundation of fluffy white vapor. When we drove through, a hazy mist enveloped the local scenery, coating the tall pines and creating an ethereal paradise.

Our coolest event, by far, was the Albuquerque International Balloon Fiesta. This is the most photographed event in the world, according to Kodak. We weren't actually working at the fiesta, but did retail stops around the occasion; however, nothing was going to stop Ali and me from attending.

To make the most of the Balloon Fiesta, you have to arrive at four in the morning. That's when the first hot-air balloons are sent up to check the morning winds. And you have to put up with bitter cold, insane crowds, and long lines at the breakfast burrito stands. But the effort is well worth it for the chance to see more than seven hundred colorful balloons bobbing across the clear blue New Mexico sky.

Putting aside the sheer quantity of inflatables, the inventiveness is what truly boggles the eye. *Look! Up in the sky! It's the Jesus Christ balloon floating next to a helium-filled Jim Beam bottle.* There was also an elephant balloon, an upside-down balloon, a bear balloon, and about 695 others.

Ali and I tried desperately to get a ride in a hot-air balloon. We begged and bargained with the Tony the Tiger balloon crew, promising

them whistles, shirts, and even a ride in the world-famous Wienermobile. But they didn't bite. It's one of the few times that a Wienermobile
couldn't get us everything we wanted.

Joining us at the Southern New Mexico State Fair in Las Cruces is
Hotdogger Leah (a.k.a. Lettuce Leah). She is on break from the Food
Service team and enthusiastically jumps in to help us out. The Southern New Mexico State Fairgrounds are a hot, barren wasteland. We're
parked in the middle of a dirt field, which wouldn't be so bad except
that today the forecast calls for apocalyptic winds. These gusts come up
unexpectedly, blowing over our table and covering us all in a thick layer
of earth. It's like a scene from *The Grapes of Wrath*.

Leah's had a rough go on the road. While Ali and I have been
blessed with a bountiful schedule, she's been trapped in a Food Service
nightmare.

The Food Service Department deals with places that sell cooked
Oscar Mayer products. Every year, they commandeer a Wienermobile
to service certain accounts. Instead of doing Share the Smiles, Leah and
her partner Derrick have been visiting movie theaters, convenience
stores, gas stations, fast-food restaurants, and flea markets. It hasn't
been fun.

"At first it sounded like we got picked for the super cool tour, coast
to coast, when in reality it was more like the Oscar Mayer Obligation
Tour," complains Leah.

To make matters worse, Leah and Derrick were driving BOLOGNA,
the runt of the '88 litter. BOLOGNA broke down their very first day, strand-
ing them on a freeway in Chicago during rush hour. The state highway
police came, as did the local media. Another time, BOLOGNA croaked
while they were giving a ride to a raffle winner.

"Has it really been that bad?" I ask Leah.

"I tried to quit, but Russ wouldn't let me," she says.

"What happened?" asks Ali.

"Well, we were cruising down the Strip in Vegas, which was a bad idea. It was probably 105 degrees out and the Wienermobile starts overheating. And it's literally spewing coolant on tourists. So people are flipping us off, there's no way we can move, and people are punching the car. We finally pull off into a hotel because we wanted to stop spewing antifreeze on people. This whole scene erupted, people being pissed off the car was smoking everywhere. I literally grabbed my suitcase and started walking to the airport and I told Derrick, 'You're on your own! I can't take it anymore! I can't take it!'"

"Oh my god," says Ali.

"I know. So then I'm rolling my bag to the airport, dripping with sweat, and I called Russ and I'm like, 'I quit. I'm walking to the airport.' And he's like, 'Sit down, take a deep breath, call me back in twenty minutes.' My mom was all ready to buy me a plane ticket home. But I ended up calling Russ back and was like, 'I'm sorry, that's terrible. I can't leave Derrick.' So I went back."

Russ eventually agreed to start shipping BOLOGNA to events. "I think I've spent more time at Penske than I have promoting the Wienermobile," says a clearly exhausted Leah.

Ali and I share a look. There but for the grace of Russ go we . . .

CHAPTER 21

There are plenty of good cities to be stranded in. Phoenix is not one of them. It's a lot of nothingness surrounded by steam.

Ali and I just survived a stint at the Arizona State Fair (theme: "Hell on Earth"). It was three days of standing on asphalt in one-hundred-degree heat while dealing with the biggest crowds we've ever seen. Totals for day one were a staggering 450 pictures, 80 Beanie Wienies, $892 raised, and more than 1,200 whistles passed out. Imagine the video game Space Invaders but with sweaty customers instead of pixilated aliens.

We now have some unexpected days off as OUR DOG gets a new transmission. It must be a complex operation because we've been without a Wienermobile for more than a week now. Each new day brings the same vague status report from Penske: "We're workin' on her. Should be ready soon."

Headquarters hates that we're just sitting around our hotel, counting the hours until the complimentary happy hour. At first, Joy tried to salvage our schedule by making us drive the rental car to some grocery stores and passing out whistles. That didn't go so well.

Being a Hotdogger without a Wienermobile is like being a cop without a badge, gun, uniform, police car, or authority. People just don't give you the same kind of respect. Store managers kept telling us to move our Mustang out of the fire lane, and the only customers who made eye contact were the ones who wanted to give us dirty looks. Joy quickly canceled the rest of our events.

Ali and I now have nothing but free time. So far, we've wandered downtown, toured Bank One Ballpark, and baked cookies. And that was just day one!

But not everything is sunny in Phoenix. Right now, there is the definite problem of too much togetherness. Ali and I have always gotten along well, but we need to take a break and see other people. Only there aren't any other people.

For the first time, cracks are starting to show in our team's rock-solid façade. With no other entertainment, we spend hours pushing each other's buttons, waiting to see who'll get hurt first.

"Don't you have any other swimsuits?" I say to Ali when she shows up at the pool in her usual green ensemble. "I'm not so sure puke green is your color."

"That's an interesting haircut," says Ali when I return from the mall with a slightly uneven head of hair. She breaks down laughing before she can even get to more insults.

One morning at breakfast I tell her, "You're getting paid to smile and look pretty. And you're only doing one of those right."

Sometimes we're mad at each other for absolutely no reason. A few days ago we took our rental car to Vegas. What should have been a celebratory side trip turned into a silent, five-hour drive. Why didn't we talk? Because Ali was twenty minutes late that morning and I got huffy. Too bad we didn't spend more time on partner-conflict resolution at Hot Dog High.

I've often wondered how they put a Wienermobile team together, but according to Russ, there's no exact science. It's more touchy-feely than anything. Part of it is educational background; part of it is personality. They don't want to put two aggressive people with each other.

However, conflict is inevitable when you put two or more Type A people in an enclosed space and then force them to be together for eighteen hours a day. Not even married couples spend this much time together.

Our general mood brightens considerably when we get word that the Wienermobile is repaired and ready to share more smiles. Work will surely bring Ali and me back together.

Our first event off the disabled list is a Pumpkin Fest in suburban Phoenix. Costumed kids picking pumpkins . . . it should be adorable.

We arrive just before opening. Ali parks the rented Mustang out front while I dock the Wienermobile. After months of being hidden in a corner by fair managers (more like "unfair" managers), we're finally granted a prime patch of real estate right off the main entrance. Headliners at last.

Those fine feelings don't last long. After parking, I walk to the back of the dog and notice a gaping hole where the television should be.

Ali walks up. "See if you notice anything different," I say.

She peers in. "I don't know. What?"

"Our TV's gone."

Ali does a double take. "Oh my God, you're right!"

Since I doubt the TV fell out, I call the Penske manager and report the news. "Hi, we just picked up the Wienermobile from you and it seems that our TV's missing."

The manager is slow to respond. "You're sure the TV's gone?"

"Yes. We have no TV."

"Hmmm, that's strange." A long pause while he ponders his next move. "Well, I'll look into it." Click.

For the moment, we're forced to put the TV tragedy behind us so we can start spreading some Halloween cheer. Ali, ever the careful planner, meticulously surveys the scene. "Why don't you bring out the tables and I'll set up the flags?"

"The flags? Really? You want to use the flags?" I can't believe she wants to use the flags.

Each Wienermobile comes complete with a cheap, highly portable form of crowd control—a string of plastic flags. Yes, nothing deters an angry mob like flapping, multicolored triangles. If only we had placed them around the Wienermobile while it was in the shop, we might still have our television.

I think the flags are a tacky eyesore. Also, there's nothing with which to hold them up. So anytime you want to break out the bunting, you must also scavenge the Wienermobile for support beams. You'd think Oscar Mayer could spare a few poles, but instead we're left to MacGyver a temporary solution. Usually we tie one end of the flag string to our table, loop it around a tree, then around the rearview mirror, across the buns, around another tree, and back to the other side of the table, thus creating a geometric shape that has yet to be named. It ends up looking pretty sad.

To me, the flags create a closed environment that doesn't invite friendly interactions. We're collecting donations here, not running a colorful prison camp.

Today, the idea is even more ridiculous because we don't even have the luxury of trees. This is Arizona. There are no trees.

I explain the situation to Ali. As usual, she's quick with an answer. "We can use the stepladder in the Wienermobile."

I'm outraged. "A stepladder? That'll look awful."

"No, it won't," she replies.

"Yes, it will. And why do we even need the flags?" I ask. "We'll probably get twenty people today."

"I think it's going to get busy," says Ali.

"Ali, it's stupid to put up the flags. We don't need them." Calling an Ali idea "stupid" is the quickest way to set her off. She hates being dismissed offhand like that. And people think I don't understand women.

Ali plants her hands on her hips, a sure sign she won't back down. "Well, I'm going to put up the flags. You can just watch."

And off she goes, storming into the Wienermobile and emerging seconds later with a fistful of flags. She spikes them on the ground and returns to retrieve the battered stepladder. Instinctively, I seek cover.

With Ali busy in the background, I set up our table and donation box. A few minutes later, I turn around to survey the damage. The boundary is ridiculously arbitrary and the rickety stepladder almost tips over under the weight of the flags. I was right—it looks awful.

A bit too giddy in my Pyrrhic victory, I let out a laugh. Ali, just finished with her masterpiece, is not amused. She shoots me a fiery glare and walks off, leaving her flapping fortress behind.

I have no idea where she's gone until I spot her on the other side of the chain-link fence, heading for the rental car. For a second, I fear she's going to flee. But instead she opens the trunk and pulls out a box of Wienermobile placemats. These floppy, plastic keepsakes are a big hit with the consumers, but they're packed in boxes that weigh about fifty pounds. At this moment, Ali couldn't care less about the bulk. She is determined to prove something.

Ali heaves the box from the trunk and wobbles toward the fence. It's painfully clear where this is heading: Ali plans to heave a fifty-pound box over a six-foot fence. I'm pretty sure that's an Olympic event. A bigger, more sensitive man would put aside his pride, deflate his inflated ego, and rush to help. Me? I angle to get a better view.

Ali soon reaches the fence, her expression an inspiring blend of fatigue and sheer will. She plants her legs and bends her knees to get a strong base. A few deep breaths follow—in and out, in and out. I notice that I'm not the only one watching this. For a moment, the Pumpkin Fest pauses, everyone transfixed by the world's strongest woman.

With one quick and determined motion, Ali jerks the box over her head. She holds it aloft, arms quivering, sweat forming on her face. From a safe distance, I admire both her form and her desire. She might actually pull this off.

Then again . . . no.

Everything unravels rather quickly. Unable to press so much weight, Ali tilts forward and the box falls from her grip, cascading down the steel fence before finally splattering on the ground. Our precious placemats spill out and begin fluttering away.

Winded, and with plastic reminders of her folly littering the parking lot, Ali glances up and sees me staring at her. Actually, she sees me laughing at her. We don't speak for the rest of the day.

Turns out, Ali was right about the flags. The crowds remain thick all day and we end up taking 550 pictures, beating our Arizona State Fair record. We leave the Wienermobile at the Pumpkin Fest and Ali drives us back to the hotel in the rental car. The silence is suffocating.

I'm nonconfrontational to a fault. I'll duck, hide, sleep—anything to avoid a fight. Arguments just make me feel . . . icky. That's why it takes a few miles before I can summon enough courage to talk to my partner.

"Ali, I'm really sorry about today. You were right about the flags."

"Thanks," she says in her most curt, sarcastic tone. "I know."

Ali then tightens her grip on the steering wheel and stays focused on the road. I feel like more of an ass with each passing mile. Internally, I curse my controlling nature and distaste for compromise. When there are only two of you, winning 100 percent of the time means the other person loses 100 percent of the time. This would be a great monologue to share with Ali, but there's no way to speak now. The gulf between us is too big.

We arrive back at the hotel and go straight to our rooms. There are few things sadder than sitting alone on Friday night. When a partner is your only way out of a cramped hotel room, it's probably smart to keep on her good side. Mercifully, Ali is not one to hold a grudge and in the morning it's like the whole flag incident never happened.

Just to be safe, I offer to drive.

CHAPTER 22

One of the lesser-known consequences of World War II was that gas rationing forced the Wienermobile off the road. Oscar Mayer provided canned meats for soldiers overseas, but war-weary citizens were in no mood for a tiny chef riding around in an oversized sausage.

After the war, Oscar Mayer went on a rapid expansion that included buying plants in Philadelphia and Los Angeles. What had been a regional company was now national. The Wienermobile returned, with five new vehicles built between 1950 and 1953. These Wienermobiles were designed and built by custom car company Gerstenlager of Wooster, Ohio, on a Dodge chassis. They were sent to cities that had Oscar Mayer meat-processing plants.

"They were pretty basic vehicles, just an engine on a frame and that was it," says former Oscar Mayer sales manager Tom Phillips.

In those days, the Wienermobiles were serviced at Oscar Mayer maintenance facilities. "At every plant they would have a garage where we kept our delivery trucks," says Phillips. "So we would do the maintenance that we could do at our garage. Or, if it was a bigger job, we would just send it to somebody local and have it done."

There were no Hotdoggers back in 1950, so Oscar Mayer either hired a driver or recruited someone from sales to take Little Oscar around. Joe Kossack, who worked in the Chicago office, recalls how the system worked. "It was not my regular job. I was a service salesman. I drove a truck, and I originally sold Oscar Mayer products off the truck. So I was familiar with that kind of driving. That's probably why they chose me to drive the thing around." Kossack says he would find out Little Oscar's itinerary and visit the stores beforehand, putting up posters that advertised the Wienermobile's upcoming visit.

While Phillips remembers that these Wienermobiles "held up quite well," Kossack says that "the old ones used to break down quite a bit." But at least they "looked terrific on the outside," according to Kossack.

Also looking terrific on the outside was company founder Oscar F. Mayer. When he turned ninety-five, Oscar was asked if he was going to retire. "I haven't any plans for that. Of course, I don't spend so much time here at the plant anymore, only a few hours a day. Some Saturdays I don't come down at all."

But Oscar F. couldn't go on forever. He died on March 11, 1955, just eighteen days before his ninety-sixth birthday. His son, Oscar G. Mayer, succeeded him as chairperson. Grandson Oscar G. Mayer Jr. was elected company president.

Despite the corporate changes, the Wienermobile rolled on. In 1958, the advertising icon was put in the hands of a design icon—Brooks Stevens. For most people, redesigning the Oscar Mayer Wienermobile would be a professional triumph. For Brooks Stevens, it was a career footnote.

Brooks Stevens was an innovative and influential industrial designer who created more than three thousand products, including the first electric steam iron, the first motor home, and the first electric clothes dryer with a glass window. Looking for a more futuristic Wienermobile, Oscar Mayer commissioned Stevens to design it. Stevens, who once said, "There's nothing more aerodynamic than a wiener," was the perfect man for the job.

The 1958 Wienermobile was the product of a forward-thinking individual. Building with fiberglass on a Willys Jeep chassis (which he also designed), Stevens created the Wienermobile's "classic shape" by, as he said, "putting the wiener in the bun." As the Milwaukee Art Museum noted in an exhibit of Stevens's work, "previously the vehicle had been a low, inelegant truck with a giant hot dog riding atop it." After Stevens, the Wienermobile would truly resemble the object it was trying to represent.

Stevens introduced a bubble-nose cockpit that occupied the front of the vehicle. The driver and Little Oscar were now on full display, rather than hidden behind narrow windows.

Oscar Mayer built five of the 1958 Wienermobiles. When the vehicle came up for a redesign in 1969, Oscar Mayer brought the project back in-house. Oscar Mayer mechanics, working at company headquarters in Madison, cobbled together two more Wienermobiles using whatever parts they could find. The 1969 models cost about $60,000 each. They abandoned the bubble-nose cockpit in favor of the wraparound windows last seen on the 1952 version. The buns, however, remained.

The 1969 design was replicated in 1975. This time, the Wienermobile was built on a 1973 Chevy motor home chassis by Plastic Products of Milwaukee. "A huge block of styrene foam was carved to wiener and bun shape and hollowed to create a skeleton for the fiberglass that was sprayed over it to form the $75,000 vehicle." The 1975 Wienermobile wasn't on the road for long, however. In 1977, the program was suddenly discontinued. Forty-one years after making its debut on the streets of Chicago, the Wienermobile was dead.

CHAPTER 23

I t's November 4 and I'm still in shorts. Maybe I *will* miss Phoenix.

Ali and I have been here for one month. While other teams are busy gallivanting across the country, we've built a peaceful, if sometimes uneasy, home at the Residence Inn. The long layover has been a welcome diversion from our usual nomadic lifestyle, allowing us to plant some rather shallow roots. It seems like we're finally residents, not just tourists. That feeling of permanence is comforting. I had forgotten how much I missed the small things—grocery shopping, cooking my own meals, knowing where all the adult bookstores are . . .

But everything is temporary with the Wienermobile, and now a new mission awaits: the Share the Smiles finale. Every team and all six Wienermobiles are converging on Louisville so we can pat our backs raw in a fit of self-congratulation. Curiously, we've been told very little about the event. There will be a parade and plenty of Wienermobiles . . . that's about all we know. Oscar Mayer has suddenly gone top secret.

I'm actually surprised the company remembered to invite us. For months, Ali and I have been left alone to wander the lonely Southwest. No one from headquarters has come to visit, and no one has questioned our activities. There was hardly any fuss made about our extended stay in Phoenix or the luxury suite we split at Caesar's Palace in Las Vegas. We are the Lost Team, long gone and almost forgotten.

The office gives us four days to reach Louisville. That's ninety-six hours to travel one thousand miles in a Wienermobile that just got a new transmission. I'm sure nothing could possibly go wrong.

As it turns out, everything could possibly go wrong. I'll spare the gory mechanical details and instead stick to the highlights. It takes nine hours to drive from Phoenix to Albuquerque. A normal car could make that in six.

Getting from Albuquerque to Tulsa (a distance of five hundred miles) takes sixteen hours after we blow out a crank shaft in the no man's land of Tucumcari, New Mexico. It takes Penske two hours to find us and another two to fix the problem.

Day three is Tulsa to St. Louis. We leave our hotel at 8:30 a.m. and, five minutes later, the Wienermobile starts coughing up coolant. A Penske mechanic comes to the scene and spends an hour trying to diagnose the problem before finally giving up and towing us to the shop. After getting a new water pump, we finally leave Tulsa at 4:30 p.m. That means it took us seven hours to travel five miles. We arrive in St. Louis at 12:30 a.m., wanting nothing more than to drive our cooked sausage into the Mississippi River. And Louisville is still one day away.

By now, we're quite familiar with Wienermobile breakdowns and Penske has become like a second home. As sick as we are of visiting Penske, I think they're equally sick of us. Said one Penske mechanic after crawling under the Wienermobile in a sweltering San Diego parking lot, "I swear to god, if I ever meet the guy who signed this national contract . . ."

CHAPTER 24

We've just found out that protestors will be picketing tomorrow's parade."

Russ stands at the front of hotel conference room in downtown Louisville addressing a room of nervous, confused Hotdoggers. All the blinds are drawn, forcing everyone to squint to see our boss. A band of outside PR consultants, all dressed in black, shuffle about in the background, whispering and passing notes. For a Share the Smiles finale, not many people are smiling.

We've been anticipating the Share the Smiles finale for months. It was supposed to be part celebration, part reunion, and part farewell. It doesn't look like they'll be much celebration now, but at least all the Hotdoggers are back together. My arms are already sore from all the hugging.

Brad and Sofia look happy, tan, and well rested. Love on the road seems to agree with them. But their relationship is in for a dramatic change because this event is the last for the holdovers from Hotdoggers XI. Those wily veterans who helped guide us down the hot dog highways are being forced to grow up and find real jobs. I don't envy them. Brad will soon have to hand in his American Express card, his Penske keychain, and his Sofia.

"What are you going to do next?" I ask him.

"Hang out, maybe travel down to South America. I'll figure something out." It's typical Brad—not a worry in the world.

"What about you and Sofia?"

"I don't know. We'll figure something out."

More surprisingly, this is also the end of the road for the Food Service team of Derrick and Leah. They were originally hired for a six-month stint, but are being let go early because Oscar Mayer spent so much money transporting (more like towing) their broken-down Wienermobile from event to event. They're being paid until January, which is nice, but no one wants to see Derrick and Leah go.

I ask Derrick how he feels about the sudden news. "Kind of devastated. I figured we were going to be doing this for a year."

We don't see much of Russ or the PR posse after the meeting. They spend the rest of the evening huddled in the war room, drawing up contingency parade plans. Rumors fly that we're canceling the event and sneaking out of town. But then late word comes down that the parade is going on as planned. It's Oscar Mayer versus the protestors. To the winner goes the publicity.

Game day starts insanely early. By 6 a.m., all Hotdoggers are dressed in their flight suits and waiting in the hotel lobby. No one's peppy, but Sofia and Brad look especially tired.

Russ hands out the assignments. Luke, the Ice Man of Wienermobile drivers, is tapped to pilot the lead parade vehicle. I'll be driving the fourth Wienermobile in line. It's not a glamorous position, but it beats running and tossing out whistles.

Once we know our roles, all Hotdoggers are herded into nondescript white vans that ferry us to our vehicles. Ever since the protest threat emerged, this event has gone from publicity stunt to military operation.

That level of precision continues once we get to the Wienermobile staging area. All the important people (Russ, the head of

Second Harvest, the PR people) are packed into the lead Wienermobile. The rest of the invited guests are sprinkled throughout
the remaining Wienermobiles. I'm not sure who the middle-aged
couple in my Wienermobile are; they could be just some random
tourists picked off the street. But they are certainly excited about
the parade.

"Ooooh . . . look!" says the wife. "Ketchup carpet!"

Before we begin, Russ lines us up for final instructions. We're to
drive slowly and with extreme caution. We're to appear happy and energetic, as if nothing in the world was wrong.

Most importantly, we're to remain ever vigilant against any
impending threats. We don't know where, when, or how they'll strike,
but it's fairly certain that something is going down. As an added precau-
tion, our route has been trimmed from six blocks to three, meaning that
the parade will last about ten minutes.

Russ distributes two-way radios to each team and we're off, ready
to dazzle sleepy downtown Louisville.

I soon feel silly calling this a "parade." Sure, we've got a police
escort and a few road closures, but there is no crowd and certainly no
excitement. The only people we pass are confused pedestrians on their
way to lunch. At least they'll have an interesting story to tell tonight.
"Honey, you'll never guess what happened to me today. I was walking
down the street and suddenly six Wienermobiles drove by. No, I don't
know what they were doing. Yeah, and then I met up with Sam for lunch.
Ordered the chicken salad."

Being fourth wiener in line, there's not much for me to do. In the
back, my passengers wave at invisible crowds while I follow the bun in
front of me and try not to doze off. The two-way radio rests awkwardly
in my cup holder, crackling with static and occasional barks from Russ.
It's quiet for a parade. Too quiet.

I decide this is a good time to lighten the mood. I pick up the walkie
and, in mock horror, whisper, "I see Wienermobiles."

Everyone laughs . . . except for Russ. "David, this is not a time for joking."

Chastised, I go back to silently following the Wienermobile in front of me. Just as I'm settling into a nice parade trance, the pork hits the fan.

"Pig in the street!" blares the radio. "Pig in the street!"

I slam on the brakes and instinctively duck behind the wheel. My passengers drop their smiles and rush to the front of the cabin. They'll be no more waving today.

"There's a pig in the street? Where? What's going on?"

"I don't know!"

The radio goes strangely silent and the protruding wiener in front of me makes it impossible to see what's going on. Suddenly, a blur of blue passes us. It's a line of police rushing to the scene. I'm guessing that pig didn't get loose accidentally.

As we continue to wait and wonder, Russ's commanding voice comes over the radio. "Everybody just keep going. Continue the route."

I want to pick up the radio and scream, *Continue the route? Are you crazy? We're sitting ducks out here!* But, trying to be brave for my passengers, I dutifully drive on.

It's not long before we see what caused the commotion.

Off to our left, police are handcuffing a man in a bright-pink pig costume. He's not struggling so much as doing an angry dance of dissension, his giant pig head swaying back and forth as the cops pull back his furry arms. A MEAT IS MURDER sign rests at his feet.

"Oh, good heavens," says the wife.

The parade continues, although the flailing, fluffy pig has stolen most of our thunder. My passengers are dumbstruck. As am I. This is the first time I've ever been protested.

After finishing the parade, we all converge on Luke. As lead driver, he was right there, staring into the swine's soul. Luke, a few shades paler than when I saw him last, is eager to share his story.

"I had Russ sitting there with me and I had Cyndi [Oscar Mayer's head of PR], who was a basket case. And it was one of those '95's where the gas and brake are very close together on the right side of the wheel shaft . . . you had to turn your foot sideways so you didn't hit both."

We all nod in sympathy. Luke continues: "We're driving along and I see the pig coming out and Russ says, 'Slow to a stop. Slow to a stop.' And I quickly went to stop, but instead of hitting the brake, I hit the gas."

Luke came within inches of running over the man-pig. A collective gasp ripples through the audience.

"I got much closer than I should have. The pig came up and started banging on the hood. Then, the pig laid down in front of the Wienermobile until the cops came and pulled him away."

We all take turns congratulating Luke on his Hotdogger heroism. This man single-handedly saved the parade. Imagine the headlines if he had splattered a protester.

In the end, the pig didn't accomplish much. The few media outlets that covered the finale either ignored the protest or buried it deep in the story. For once, it was a good thing that Oscar Mayer threw a publicity party and nobody showed up.

The old gang is all hanging out in Madison for a few days before Thanksgiving break. The big news is that headquarters is shuffling the teams again, I think in an effort to keep partners from killing each other.

Ali and I hit a few bumps, but never came close to physical violence. And that's good because I think she could take me in a fight. Really, our only big argument involved flags and, in hindsight, was totally my fault. Actually, I'm sure most of our disagreements were probably my fault.

My disappointment over losing Ali is somewhat tempered when I learn that my new partner is actually my old partner—Sofia. Yes, I'm reuniting with the former love of my life. Maybe I finally have a shot now that Brad is done with the program and on an extended vacation in the jungles of South America. Hey, a kid can dream.

CHAPTER 25

Our new territory is the South. We'll be starting in North Carolina and then working toward the Gulf of Mexico. Joy hands out our schedules and I eagerly skim the calendar, eager to know what fair or festival I'll be attending next.

"This is amazing!" I accidentally blurt out, attracting some snide looks from my fellow Hotdoggers. I'm looking at perhaps the greatest itinerary in Hotdogger history—a month in Atlanta for Super Bowl promotions, then the Daytona 500, then Mardi Gras. This type of schedule deserves an acceptance speech.

While I'm basking in my good fortune, Ali walks over and tosses her schedule at me. I look it over and almost wince. She's spending a long winter working the frozen Midwest. Even worse, most of her events are in and around Madison. Quite a letdown after months out west.

I hand her my sheet and then lean back in anticipation of her envy.

"I hate you," she says after looking over my schedule.

Advantage Ihlenfeld.

"So how's everything going with Brad? You guys still talk?" I breathlessly ask Sofia during our first drive together as reunited teammates.

Before we separate for Christmas break, the office has assigned us to help with the Madison Toys for Tots drive.

"We talk," she responds. "Things are still going good."

"Oh . . . you mean you're still going out?" I ask in my most casual tone.

"Well, I don't know what you'd call it, but, yeah, I guess."

"So you're dating. That's cool."

"Yeah, we'll see. I think he may come visit us on the road."

That's terrible. "That's great!"

"Yeah," says Sofia with a smile. "Who would have thought?"

"Not me."

It takes me a bit longer to load the Wienermobile with toys, what with my rebroken heart. But after slowly stuffing the back of the cabin, I drive us to the National Guard Armory. I turn onto the armory road, not paying attention to anything but the fact that it's going to be a long time before I see another woman naked.

Suddenly, quick bursts of red and blue light up the side mirror. "Great," I moan, "We're being pulled over again."

The Wienermobile may not attract chicks, but it's a big hit with the cops. I watch the officer approach with a Terminator-like swagger. He takes his time, soaking up the experience.

"Sofia, can you go to the back and get the guy some whistles? Hopefully he won't want a picture."

At last, the officer is at my side window. "Hello, officer," I begin. "Would you like a—"

"License and registration, please," the cop says.

"Oh . . . yes, officer," I stammer. "Right away." I'm dumbfounded. This man doesn't seem to be a fan.

I pull out my driver's license while Sofia scours the hot dog dash for something resembling the registration. We've never had to prove that this thing is actually registered. After a frantic search, Sofia comes up with the documents and I hand everything over for inspection.

The cop methodically studies the papers. "Who does this vehicle belong to?" he asks.

This guy can't be serious. Even if you lived in some sad, hot dog-less world, it still says Oscar Mayer in giant letters on the side.

"Oscar Mayer," I respond. He lets out an unimpressed grunt.

I try playing the good citizen card. "We were just delivering toys to the armory," I say, motioning to the giant building in front of us.

He doesn't seem too impressed. "You were going forty in a twenty-five," he says. "That's pretty fast."

The pure spectacle of a cop interrogating the driver of the Wiener-mobile brings a few National Guardsmen out onto the lawn. Like me, they're not quite sure what to make of the scene.

The officer takes my license and registration back to his car.

"Is he going to give me a ticket?" I ask Sofia.

"I don't know."

The officer takes his time, letting me simmer in my own guilty juices. When he does finally return, he hands me a hot pink ticket and then wordlessly retreats to his squad car. I sit frozen, feeling like the worst Hotdogger in the world.

"That sucks," says Sofia.

"Uh huh," is all I can respond with.

We eventually drive the four feet to the armory and drop off the toys to some sympathetic Guardsmen. "I can't believe that guy gave you a ticket!" says one.

Our good deed done, we have to return to headquarters. Sofia drives this time.

That night, I spend a long time staring at the large, white phone in my hotel room. I have to call Russ and break the news. This isn't something you leave on voicemail or bury in an e-mail. The one positive is that Russ is on vacation and can't hit me through the phone.

When I finally work up the courage to tell Russ about the ticket, he sounds more disappointed than angry. I'd much prefer anger.

"That is not how we want our company represented," he says. "Especially in Madison."

Russ lectures me on the importance of vehicle safety and reminds me that I am the public face of Oscar Mayer and it is my responsibility to present the company in a positive light. He also orders me to write a letter explaining what happened and what I'll do differently in the future.

"All right. I'm really sorry about this, Russ."

"Let's just make sure we don't have a repeat of this incident." And with that, Russ hangs up.

This is not how I wanted to spend my Christmas vacation, sitting in a doctor's office, trying to explain a pain in the ass.

"When did the pain start?"

"A few weeks ago."

"Have you noticed any change in appetite?"

"No."

"Any weight loss?"

"No."

"Any blood in your stool?"

"Um, a little . . . yes."

That gets his attention. "I see." The doctor scribbles down some notes on his clipboard. "And what do you do for a living?"

"I, uh, drive the Oscar Mayer Wienermobile."

"You do what?"

"Drive the Wienermobile. It's like a big hot dog on wheels."

"I see," he says while scribbling some more.

The doctor schedules me for a colonoscopy.

"What does that involve?" I ask.

"They'll insert a small camera in your rectum to check for any problems." That sounds refreshing.

I'm quite nervous the night before my procedure. What if there's something seriously wrong with me? What if it's cancer? Or some sort of tumor? Is this the end of my Hotdogger career?

No healthy twenty-two-year-old should have to get a camera up the butt. That's something elderly men look forward to. To make matters worse, I have to drink a gallon of medicated liquid in order to "flush out my pipes." The clear fluid tastes like bleach, making it difficult to drink without gagging. But it sure does work. I spend most of the night within eyesight of a bathroom, just waiting for the familiar pains to start.

The procedure starts early in the morning. As terrible as a colonoscopy sounds, it's not so bad. Being heavily sedated certainly helps. The doctor pumps me full of gas and I happily drift off to a happy place beyond cameras and rectums. I wake up an hour later, dazed and just a bit sore.

A few days later, I return for the results. I don't have cancer. But I do have hemorrhoids.

"You need more fiber," advises the doctor. "Oh, and try not to sit so much."

CHAPTER 26

The Wienermobile program was unceremoniously dumped in 1977. There were a few reasons behind the demise of this advertising icon. First, the vehicles were old and proving expensive to maintain. Then there was the continued rise of television advertising. The Wienermobile still grabbed people's attention, but it had a very limited range. Just compare the number of consumers you can reach from a few hours spent in a Piggly Wiggly parking lot versus a thirty-second TV ad.

Television made stars out of such corporate faces as Ronald McDonald and Tony the Tiger. Sales manager Tom Phillips saw firsthand how marketing was changing. "We did not do a lot of promoting to the public with Little Oscar, so he kind of got lost with some of the other characters who were out there." The Wienermobile and Little Oscar may have been revolutionary in 1936, but forty years later they were sadly out of date.

Phillips sums up all the problems associated with the Wienermobile program: "It became more difficult to schedule Little Oscar with retailers and it became more difficult to find people to fill that role. And it became a growing expense. So all those things put together, not any one of them, were responsible for the demise of the program."

Mothballing the Wienermobile fleet was just the latest injustice against the hot dog. Consumer advocate Ralph Nader said hot dogs were "among America's deadliest missiles" and even testified before Congress about their dangers. In 1972, Time ran an essay titled "The Decline and Fill of the American Hot Dog" in which the author suggested that the golden age of the hot dog could be coming to an end. "Those who see the hot dog as an American symbol may be discomfited to learn that its very ethos is vanishing. Once, for example, franks were the staple of daytime World Series games. But this year, all weekday Series games will be played at night. Who wants a hot dog after dinner?"

Phyllis Lovrien thought the hot dog was getting a bad break. And she was in a position to do something about it. Lovrien became Oscar Mayer's vice president of marketing the same year the Wienermobile was taken off the road. She remembers the time as only a marketing executive can. "The hot dog was getting overlooked as a good food," says Lovrien. "It was time to go back and revisit what we could do to highlight the attributes of the brands as well as the product line."

Lovrien developed a public relations campaign that showed the ingredients in a one-pound package of wieners. The ads succeeded because they demystified the hot dog, but Lovrien wasn't satisfied. She went to Oscar Mayer president Jim McVey with a bold proposal: bring back the Wienermobile. According to Lovrien, McVey's response was a curt "no way."

Other Oscar Mayer executives weren't enthusiastic about reviving the Wienermobile either. "They all said, 'Leave it alone, it's dead, it's gone, we don't need to do this.'" says Lovrien. "They didn't view it as an icon. They thought of it as a sales promotion. And there's a big difference. When I could point out the tangible benefits of leveraging the difference, then that made it very appealing for them."

Lovrien finally persuaded her bosses to bring back two Wienermobiles in celebration of the vehicle's fiftieth anniversary in 1986. If the tour was a success, Oscar Mayer president Jim McVey agreed to consider reviving the Wienermobile program.

A 1965 Wienermobile, old Number 7, was brought out, dusted off, and sent on the road for the summer. Fueled by a wave of nostalgia, the Wienermobile's return was a big hit. Large crowds showed up at appearances and the company was flooded with requests to see the legendary frank. The tour was successful enough that Oscar Mayer did it again the next summer.

The only problem was that you couldn't really drive Number 7. "It was a beast," recalls Russ. "It was just more for show than for go. It didn't really have a window that opened; it had little pivoting pieces of fiberglass that dropped down. So if you were paying tolls, it was just atrocious. They ended up getting a truck and a trailer and basically hauling it around."

After seeing that the public still had an appetite for the Wienermobile, Oscar Mayer executives decided that it was time to bring back the program. There was just one catch—the company wouldn't pay anyone to work on the project. To get the Wienermobile back on the road, Phyllis Lovrien would have to rely on a staff composed completely of volunteers.

"When Jim [McVey] said 'great' on the Wienermobile, all of a sudden I had this big job and nobody to do it," Lovrien says. "People heard about it and they'd come knock on my door and say, 'You know what, I'm in the garage out here and we can help you with this. I have time, I can fit it in.' I had volunteers like that from all over the place."

One of the first to sign on was Russ Whitacre. "Russ was an HR guy who did training in the personnel department," remembers Lovrien. "He came and said, 'Hey, you're going to need to do some training of these Hotdoggers. Let me design a training system for you.'"

Lovrien also remembers Joy jumping on the bandwagon right away. "Joy came and said, 'I love the Wienermobile and I would do anything you want me to do and I will do it on my own time.'"

After getting executive approval and rounding up a volunteer staff, Lovrien had just one minor concern left: Who could possibly build these new Wienermobiles?

CHAPTER 27

The Oscar Mayer Wienermobile is in my driveway. Viewed from the street, the up-swooping orange dog eclipses half the house. It's quite a surreal sight.

My family lives in Naperville, Illinois, about thirty miles west of Chicago. Naperville is like a Norman Rockwell painting come to life—kids bound across well-manicured lawns, neighbors mingle at festive block parties, and the former mayor is best known as Officer Friendly (seriously).

Looking back, my childhood was ridiculously idyllic. Dinner was always on the table by six, and my brother and I had a big backyard in which to play football and freeze tag, and run bases. My parents never fought, or, if they did, they made sure we didn't hear it. Summers were divided between swim team and our lakefront cottage in northern Wisconsin.

I can't remember any real problems growing up, which is probably why I'm ill-prepared to deal with even slight adversity now. I'm so used to things being perfect that I have trouble adjusting if they're not.

"You're taking the Wienermobile to Beebe tomorrow," says my mom after I've been in the door for only a few minutes.

"What?!"

"You have to," my mom insists. "They're all looking forward to it."

"You already told everyone I was coming? Why did you do that?"

Beebe is my elementary school alma mater, the place where I learned to play the recorder, write cursive, and make pinecone Christmas ornaments. I don't see the need to revisit it, especially when I could be sitting in the basement catching up with my Nintendo.

"David James!" My mom rarely uses my middle name. Whenever she does, I know I've lost.

"Fine. I'll take it to Beebe."

While my brother and I forgot about Beebe the second we left, my mom still has a strong connection to the school. When I was in high school, she got tired of the stay-at-home routine and took a job there. For the last few years she's had two jobs at the school—monitoring the lunchroom and tutoring kids who have trouble reading. Guess which position pays more.

Now that her son is a Hotdogger, my mom is eager to show me off. I have no choice but to comply. The woman doesn't ask for much and, besides, the Hotdogger Oath requires that I never pass up a promotional opportunity.

I've driven to Beebe hundreds of times, but never in a Wienermobile. You'd be amazed at what a difference it makes. Suddenly, every turn is new and exciting. I make a left onto Washington. There's Jefferson Junior High, another Ihlenfeld alma mater. A pack of kids cut across the grass valley that leads to the school. Everyone stops as the Wienermobile rolls by, their faces frozen in that familiar "this can't be happening" look. Then a left onto East Twelfth, past Saybrook Pool, where I was a lifeguard and coach of the mighty Sharks Swim Team. This does feel pretty good . . . maybe I need to start trusting my parents more.

Moments later, I'm back on Beebe blacktop. This playground and gathering place hasn't changed much since I graduated twelve years ago. There's still the worn tetherball court and the balance beam where

I could never win a game of chicken. It all looks so familiar that even I'm surprised to see a Wienermobile parked here.

Hardened by a winter that often stretches into May, Naperville children are hearty creatures. Recess is seldom canceled by cold. Parents over-bundle their kids, making temperature control a simple matter of unlayering. I used to be like them, taunting the wind while packing snowballs with my bare hands. Cold was a fact of life; you just lived with it.

But I've gone soft. Three months in California followed by two in Arizona and New Mexico must have messed up my inner thermometer. Frostbite nibbles at my angry red extremities. My mom, her green, furry hood encircling a rosy face, seems unfazed. She's as still as a statue next to me, proudly watching her son set up.

I decide on a minimalist approach for today's impromptu show and tell—nothing but our trusty folding table, a bag of whistles, and an open gull-wing door. I've even left Sofia in her warm hotel room to spare her this ruckus scene. (Not that she volunteered to come along. She's even more cold averse than I am.) I just hope that a Wienermobile on their playground will be enough "wow" for these kids. It's no Pokemon.

My mother has suddenly morphed into a PR guru. In only a few hours she's corralled hundreds of children and faculty and set up a tight schedule. From nine to ten, I will be greeting every student at Beebe. That's kindergarten through fifth grade, hundreds of eager children, in sixty minutes. And there's also a sizeable number of teachers, administrators, janitors, and lunch ladies who also want in on the action.

And then there's my dad. Recently retired after more than thirty years of hard work, he seems a bit uneasy with his new abundance of free time. He loves projects and sees my visit as a chance to be productive again. So he spent the entire morning pitching my inspirational story to the *Chicago Tribune*, the *Chicago Sun Times*, the *Daily Herald*, and the *Naperville Sun*.

"Well, he drives the Oscar Mayer Wienermobile and this morning he's going to take it to his old elementary school," I heard him say. "I think that's something your readers would like to hear about . . ."

Amazingly, a reporter from the *Daily Herald* takes the bait and comes to ask a few questions before the crush of kids. I put on my bright Hotdogger smile, brush off my handbook on media superlatives, and provide my best Oscar Mayer–approved answers:

"This is incredible. Little did I think I'd be doing this, let alone pulling it into my driveway or onto Beebe's playground. It's a great opportunity to travel. You get to see so much of the country and the country gets to see you. Everyone gets so excited."

Another empty interview, just how we like 'em.

A few minutes later, the school doors burst open and a mass of children sprint toward the Wienermobile with such frightening velocity that I think about tipping over the table for cover. Fortunately, they come to a screeching halt inches from the vehicle. These are the first graders. Judging by their wide-open mouths, I'd say they're already fans.

I hear mumblings of glee: "Wow, this is awesome!" "It's huge!" "Look at the little camera!"

And I was worried about being cool.

When everyone settles down, I launch into my presentation. "Hi, I'm Hot Dog Dave." For the first time, that line gets a laugh.

"I actually went to Beebe many, many years ago. Now I drive across the country in the Oscar Mayer Wienermobile. Has anyone ever seen a Wienermobile before?"

A few hands go up.

"Well, the Wienermobile has been around since 1936 and right now there are six of them all around the country. This one was built in 1995 and it's called OSCAR."

"Oscar . . . Oscar," the kids giggle as they repeat the name.

"OSCAR's got relish-colored seats, a ketchup and mustard walkway, a bunroof, and a television."

There's a collective "oooh" when I mention the television.

"Now the Wienermobile is really just a big truck. Can anyone guess how much OSCAR here weighs *in hot dogs*?"

The kids quickly shout out guesses:

"Two hundred!"

"Twelve!"

"Nine billion!"

I hold up my hands to stop the bidding. "Actually, the Wienermobile weighs about one hundred thousand hot dogs."

More "ooohs" from this most captive audience. While I still have their attention, I open it up for questions.

"How fast does it go?"

"It hauls buns," I answer, recycling the old line.

"Do you sleep in there?"

"Nope, it's not a Wienie-bago."

"Does the television work?"

"Yes, it does."

"Ooooh . . ."

I ask the children to line up so they can peek in the Wienermobile and get their very own whistle. Surprisingly, they actually listen and, with the help of some talented teachers, quickly form a long, slithering line. Each child steps up, gazes inside for a second, and then grabs a whistle. Happy children—another Naperville hallmark.

The assembly-line efficiency is beautiful. Within minutes, the entire first grade is processed and gleefully tooting whistles around the playground. (Sorry, teachers.) Soon, everyone is back inside and I reload the whistle bag for round two.

The presentations pass quickly. In between groups, I find a few moments to talk to my former teachers. Most surprised to see me is Mrs. Baker, my second grade math teacher. Somehow time has not touched her. She looks exactly the same as I remembered her. Well, maybe a little shorter.

My fears about Mrs. Baker laughing off my new career are completely unfounded. Like the children, she's in awe. "This is one of the neatest things I have ever seen," she tells me while running her gloved hand across the smooth hull.

While I'm taking to Mrs. Baker, the *Daily Herald* reporter asks for her impressions.

"Who would've thought he'd end up doing this?" she says in a tone somewhere between wonder and bewilderment. "He was always a good helper and very polite. I didn't see this coming—I always thought he'd be a doctor or do something with math. But I can see why Oscar Mayer chose him."

Yes, this is about as far from being a doctor as one can get.

After the reporter is done with her, Mrs. Baker returns her attention to me. "So, what are you going to do after the Wieniemobile?"

"I don't know. Do you need any janitors?"

"You always were a funny one," says Mrs. Baker with a chuckle. "But, really, any idea what's next?"

I stare blankly at Mrs. Baker for a moment, disappointed that my joke failed to deflect her question. "Um, I honestly don't know."

"Well, you'll figure it out."

Let's hope so, Mrs. Baker.

In between classes, I look over at my beaming parents. Mom's accepting congratulations like I just became president. Dad's busy taking pictures and providing deep background to the reporter ("Make sure you mention he graduated summa cum laude from the University of Missouri"). Basking in so much love and attention does wonders for your self-esteem.

I wish I could eavesdrop on some dinner conversations tonight, when these kids will have a real answer to that oft-asked question, "Did anything exciting happen at school today?"

Once again, my mom was right. Never pass up an opportunity to show off.

CHAPTER 28

Atlanta is not a fun place in January. It's cold and unfriendly, the cityscape painted in depressing shades of gray and white. The road salt used to combat ice gets everywhere—your tires, your shoes, your soul. This city hibernates in winter because what sane person would want to be out in such a mess?

No, you don't want to visit Atlanta in January. Unless there's a Super Bowl going on and you've got a Wienermobile.

Our schedule says, "Super Bowl—Atlanta." It's right there in dot matrix black. An entire month spent canvassing the ATL, culminating in an appearance at the big game itself.

But, like so many things involving the Wienermobile, it's only an illusion. Turns out "Super Bowl—Atlanta" was never meant to be taken literally. It's just a simplification of our actual purpose. The schedule should read: "Outskirts of Atlanta—Drive to rundown grocery stores and siphon off whatever residual Super Bowl attention you can." So you can see why they had to abbreviate.

Yes, we'll be in Atlanta for the Super Bowl. Only we'll just be watching it on a hotel TV instead of in a heated luxury box, eating stale pizza rolls instead of catered beef Wellington. Dream big and settle for small, that's the Wienermobile way of life.

We won't be appearing at the Super Bowl because Kraft, which owns Oscar Mayer, isn't an official sponsor. But there's no law against doing promotions around and in no way affiliated with the Super Bowl. The proper term for such covert advertising ops is "guerilla marketing"—the corporate equivalent of party crashing.

This is my first visit to Atlanta, but Sofia is an old pro, having done a college internship at CNN en Español. Our tour of duty here lasts from January 9 until the end of the month. In that time we'll be splitting event duties with YUMMY, the Wienermobile piloted by Candace and Shawna. I'm not sure why we need to saturate the Atlanta market so heavily; it's not like the Super Bowl tourists will be arriving three weeks before the big game. But, as has been proven time and time again, I know nothing about meat-based marketing.

"Sofiiiiieee!"

"Aaaaasssssshhhhhhhllleeeeeyyyy!"

I watch as Sofia streaks toward the dark-haired stranger who just walked in the bar. This must be Ashley, Sofia's friend from when they both interned at CNN. After college, Ashley moved back to Atlanta and became a producer for the news giant. Sofia took a slightly different path.

After hugging and complimenting each other on hair, shoes, and accessories, Sofia brings her friend over to the table. "Dave, this is Ashley."

I look up from my drink. The site of this stranger wobbles my tall chair and I have to fight tumbling onto the pool table. Ashley is striking—probably the most exotic-looking white girl I've ever seen. Her long, dark locks appear constantly in motion, as if some film crew were following with an industrial fan. Long leather boots race toward her knee before disappearing under a black skirt. She walks in beauty, like the night, of cloudless climes and starry skies. Yeah, she's pretty hot.

"Hi, I'm Dave."

"I'm Ashley. So, you wanna buy me a beer?"

Well, that's bold. "Do I have a choice?"

"Not really."

One minute in and I'm already smitten. Falling in love is easy. It's all those moments afterward that I have some trouble with.

Ashley already knows about the Wienermobile, so there's no wasted time trying to explain why this qualifies as a job. We talk most of the night, one of those instant connections that seems like a drunken dream the next morning. I'm sure Ashley's met hundreds of guys like me, but I've never met anyone like her.

Ashley displays a generous amount of southern hospitality while we're in town. She shepherds us around the usual tourist haunts, gives us a tour of CNN, and even feigns interest in all things hot dog related. Not one to ever trust my initial instincts, I diligently try to find chinks in her attractive armor—a gambling problem, a facial tick, maybe an arrest record. Days of searching turn up nothing. That's a scary proposition.

It would be so much easier not to like this girl, to just leave town in a few weeks and completely forget about her, but that's impossible. We haven't even gone on a date yet, and already I'm picking out china patterns and deciding on names for our children.

Since we leave Atlanta soon, there's no time for a traditional courtship. This vagabond lifestyle forces one to accelerate the wooing process, a real problem since I was never very comfortable with regular wooing. Ashley and I make plans to watch a movie at her place. The wheels are in motion.

Unfortunately, those wheels belong to a Wienermobile. Ever since Share the Smiles ended, rental cars have become much harder to get. Which means going pretty much everywhere in the Wienermobile. Which means that you're never really off the clock. Which means I must take the company car to Ashley's. It's like Oscar Mayer is sponsoring our date.

Three wrong turns, two missed pedestrians, and several expletives later, I finally pull onto Ashley's street and spot her sprawling apartment complex. I circle the block a few times before finding a quiet, dead-end street where I can parallel park the Wienermobile in peace.

Ashley greets me at the door with a lingering hug. One minute into the evening and I'm halfway to first base. She's wearing a white apron, which seems like a solid indication that she's cooked before. Ashley leads me into her apartment, which smells of bubbling pasta and tangy tomato sauce. It's a small, rectangular place where the kitchen, living room, and bedroom are actually all the same room.

My sole contribution to dinner is a cheap bottle of chardonnay I bought at the grocery store and then smuggled onto the Wienermobile. We watch *Welcome to the Dollhouse* over a satisfying meal of spaghetti and garlic bread. It's a fine film, although only a few spots above *Eyes Wide Shut* on my list of good date movies.

After dinner, I tentatively slide toward Ashley on the couch. Food finished, bottle dry, television dark—this is my moment. I've carefully choreographed the dance in my head, fantasized about fantastic outcomes, but suddenly I can't remember a single step.

Out of nowhere, Ashley makes the first move. By yawning and rolling off the couch.

"I've got to get up early tomorrow," she says, her words emerging through a thick yawn. "Thanks a lot for coming over."

Ashley stands above me and I realize that our date is probably over.

"Oh . . . okay. Thanks for having me," I muster as I stand up from the couch of broken dreams.

I walk out on the concrete porch, the wind hitting me like a slap. I turn and look helplessly at my beautiful Ashley. Nothing says good night like an awkward staring contest.

You idiot! She's about to shut the door in your face. Do something!

I clear my throat, a few times actually. "Ashley, can I ask you something?"

Ashley leans against the doorframe and stifles another yawn. "Sure."

"Would it ruin everything if I kissed you?"

The question hangs there; I can see the words floating in front of my lips. Ashley stands frozen in front of me. Days . . . weeks . . . years pass. And then, finally, she responds in that soft, sweet voice she sometimes uses.

"We probably shouldn't. It might, you know, make things weird."

"Oh . . . okay."

"You're all over the country and who knows when I'll see you again."

"Uh huh."

"I just can't do a long-distance relationship now."

After that extensive laundry list of excuses, I want to ooze down the stairs and then run for the woods. But somehow I remain planted, a tilted smile pasted on my face.

"That's fine," I say. "I'll talk to you later then."

"Dave, I'm sorry."

By now I'm halfway down the steps, my mind already back at the hotel.

"Don't worry about it" are my parting words. I hurry back to the street, just happy to escape rejection's gravitational pull. It feels so good to be off that porch. I bound up the hill toward my car, eager to be anywhere but here.

But in my rush to escape, I've forgotten one thing—I drove to Ashley's in the Wienermobile. And now I must drive it home.

On the road, my private humiliation now seems very public. It's twenty minutes of the usual honks and waves from passing motorists. Twenty minutes of *"Hey! Nice wiener!"* Twenty minutes of red-light stares. I look straight ahead while my hands strangle the wheel. I'll be damned if I'm sharing any smiles tonight.

I pull into the hotel lot and park in a dark corner. Stepping outside, I'm immediately met by three college guys. Despite the icy weather, they're sporting torn jeans and faded T-shirts.

"Hey, do you think we could take a look inside your wiener?" says College Guy A.

I take a moment to consider. "Not tonight. Sorry."

"But—"

"Sorry."

I walk back to my room, leaving them to bob in my bitter wake.

CHAPTER 29

I'm not sure Sofia is going to make it.

She's got on every piece of Oscar Mayer clothing they gave us (pants, T-shirt, long-sleeved shirt, sweater, coat with insulated hood, gloves, wool cap) and still she's shivering like a lizard in the Antarctic. For a girl who was born in Argentina and raised in Florida, this frigid weather is a cruel shock.

"Davey, I'm freezing!" she says over and over.

After a month in Atlanta, we're finally pushing south. But even as we inch toward the equator, there's no escaping the chill. It doesn't help that the Wienermobile, in addition to having no air-conditioning, also has no heat. This becomes a serious issue on drives longer than ten minutes. Slowly hands go numb, feet tingle, and ears turn a shade of red that you can feel. The vehicle, which is a sauna in the summer, becomes an igloo in the winter. The '95s were designed to have heat, but I think it worked only for a day or two. Much like the CB radio, the hydraulic door, and the windshield wipers.

I spend some of the drive studying our schedule, which no longer looks like the greatest one in Hotdogger history. We're touring ten Walmarts in eleven days. That's more Walmarts than most people see all year. The towns we're visiting are barely visible on a map and have quaint, well-worn names like Americus, Stockbridge, and Live Oak. There's also Cordele, Valdosta, Lake City, St. Augustine, Palm Coast, and Port Orange. See if you can guess which ones are in Florida and which ones are in Georgia.

Our first stop is Fayetteville, Georgia. We pull off the highway and take a quick loop through town, hoping to glimpse the local flavor. Sadly, there isn't any. The streets are quiet and nearly deserted. A few turns later and we find the citizens—they're all at Walmart. Granted, this is not just any Walmart; this is a Super Walmart (the difference measured in both size and availability of groceries).

The Walmart parking lot is packed. But why wouldn't it be? There are only 334 shopping days until Christmas. We weave through this unexpected obstacle course, dodging carts and kids, and park in the fire lane—prime real estate that puts us right in front of the front door.

The Hotdogger job has become much less structured since Share the Smiles ended. Gone are the clearly established roles—greeter, picture taker, apron wearer. The answer to "What are you guys doing?" used to be "We're taking pictures with the Oscar Mayer Wienermobile and collecting donations for your local food bank." Now the response is more like "Um . . . we're just kinda parked here. Would you like a whistle?"

Our purpose at the Walmarts is to push product. My most repeated phrase of the day (after "It's not a chili dog") is "If you buy three Oscar Mayer products we'll give you a free beanbag toy."

Starry-eyed adults, their reluctant children in tow, approach and ask if they can go inside. "No, but you can look through the window," I tell them. It breaks my heart every time.

Sofia and I decide to work split shifts (no need for us both to suffer at the same time), so I have an hour to wander around inside the store. While browsing CDs and elastic underwear, I come to a profound conclusion: Walmart is the center of the universe.

In small towns like Fayetteville (population 11,148), Walmart is city hall, the community center, and Main Street all rolled into one. This is where people congregate, under bright fluorescent lights that bleach the skin and lay bare the soul. The retired farmers, their overalls forever worn and dusty, congregate in the frozen entrée aisle. Business deals that were once sealed over apple pie at Aunt May's Country Diner are now completed at the in-store McDonald's.

I don't know if this trend is good or bad. Sure, you lose some local flavor, but Walmart is the great equalizer. Everyone pays the same price; everyone gets the same experience. Now that's America.

Once again, the Wienermobile Department has lied to us. The schedule says "Daytona 500," and Sofia and I had looked forward to sitting in the stands, watching those cute cars zoom past. But there won't be any zooming for us. Like the Super Bowl, we won't actually be attending the big event. Instead, the office wants us to park *across the street* from the Daytona 500. It's more guerilla marketing.

So the morning of the race we get up early, drive the hour from our hotel to Daytona (all the nearby places were booked, naturally), and find a spot in the corner of the parking lot. Soon, we're joined by hundreds of revelers anxious to get to the track.

"*Hey! Hot Dog Man! How come you're not going to the race?!*"

"*That's a nice lookin' wienie!*"

"*You guys here to race?!*"

We bolt as soon as the race starts. There's no point in preaching to an empty parking lot. Desperate for a diversion, Sofia suggests driving the Wienermobile onto Daytona Beach.

"You can drive on the beach?" I ask.

"Oh, sure. I've done it tons of times."

"Yeah, but I'm not sure the Wienermobile was meant for sand."

"It'll be fine. Come on."

Well, if Sofia says so.

I turn us onto the beach and make a right at the ocean. I keep expecting someone, anyone, to run out and put a stop to this spectacle, but the locals are too busy gawking to call the police. We park next to a high-rise condo building and spend the afternoon enjoying the sun. I go for a jog, Sofia tans, and we take about a million pictures of the Wienermobile on the water.

There's a message waiting for me when we finally make it back to our hotel. "David, hello, it's Russ. Please give me a call at home when you have a moment."

He wants me to call him at home? He must know that we left the race early. And I bet someone called him about our beach stunt. Russ somehow finds out about everything that happens on the road. He covers the entire country.

I spend the next few minutes thinking up excuses and explanations, alibis and affidavits. Slowly, I dial Russ's home number, which tonight seems to be eighty-four digits long. Two rings and I start praying to the answering machine gods: *Please don't let him answer. Please let me leave a message.*

"This is Russ."

I clear my throat. "Russ, hi, it's Dave Ihlenfeld."

"David! How was the race?"

Oh god, he knows! I look around the room to make sure he's not hiding in the shower. "Well, we only saw the outside of the track, but it seemed like fun," I respond. "The parking lot certainly loved us."

"That's good to hear. You know, there's a great little seafood restaurant up that way. I'll have to send you the name when I find it."

Russ often feels compelled to showcase his encyclopedic knowledge of regional cuisine. I swear he's eaten in every town in America (and a few in Canada). One of the things he likes to do when checking into a hotel is to ask the manager where he or she would eat if they only had a few days in town. "You want to eat where the locals eat," is an oft-repeated Russ-ism.

After some forced culinary chitchat, Russ finally gets to his point. "David, we really like the work you've done, especially with media and public relations. You're putting that Missouri education to good use. You've got a good head on your shoulders, don't get rattled too easily, and have a lot of common sense. So we'd like you to go to Germany this spring."

What? Huh?

At Hot Dog High, Russ mentioned that Oscar Mayer might send two Hotdoggers on an overseas tour of U.S. military bases, but I never seriously considered myself a candidate. Actually, I'm not sure anyone considered it a real possibility. Much like air-conditioning in the Wienermobile, a European tour seemed impossible.

But now I've been offered the spot. And I have no idea what to say. "Wow?"

"Great! Thought you'd be excited. Debbie is also going over and we think you two would make a good team."

"I think we would too?" Dammit, I can't seem to put a period on my thoughts.

Although Debbie is a fellow University of Missouri grad, we never met in college and didn't exactly bond during Hot Dog High. While I was busy making sarcastic asides and drinking colorful booze out of fish bowls, Debbie was at Mass. I never got around to asking her favorite psalm, but I did find Debbie to be a genuinely nice person.

Debbie actually lived in Germany from ages eight to eleven because her Army father was stationed there. With such strong ties to the country, it's not surprising Russ picked her. My appointment, however, remains a mystery.

"Wow," I say for the second time. "This is great."

"Well, we've been impressed with your PR work and the media contacts you've generated," Russ says. "And I know you've got some German in you, so that helps."

Funny, this is the first time my German heritage has benefited me.

Ihlenfeld, besides being my last name, is also the name of both a river and a small town north of Berlin. But I don't speak the language, have never visited, and know nothing about the culture.

But today I proudly embrace my roots. They may be shallow, but they just won me a trip to Europe. I thank Russ for the opportunity and bid him "auf wiedersehen."

Feeling like a kid at Christmas, I scurry across the hall and pound on Sofia's door. She takes a few seconds to answer.

"What?" she says in a sleep-soaked voice. I'm afraid I've interrupted one of her cherished naps. But this news can't wait.

"I'm going to Europe!"

It takes a moment for Sofia to soak in what I've said. When she has, she slowly nods and then shuts the door in my face.

CHAPTER 30

*A*fter deciding to bring back the Wienermobile in 1987, Oscar Mayer was now faced with the formidable challenge of actually manufacturing the things. The company wanted six Wienermobiles built on a strict timetable. And unlike previous models, these vehicles needed to be both eye-catching and easy to maintain. The new Wienermobiles would be on the road most of the year and had to hold up under the strain of so much mileage.

Since the last Wienermobile was completed in 1976, there were very few people with practical experience manufacturing such an unusual vehicle. So Oscar Mayer decided to hire a company that did have a history with the Wienermobile: the Stevens brothers.

Brooks Stevens designed the classic '58 Wienermobile and his Mequon, Wisconsin-based company was now in the hands of his sons, Dave and Steve. "These guys had been building the Excalibur cars, which was a retro-looking, custom made, fiberglass car," says Russ Whitacre. "They were sort of inventors and tinkerers."

Phyllis Lovrien, Oscar Mayer's vice president of marketing, brought in Rick Wood, a former transportation manager at Oscar Mayer, to supervise the manufacturing. Wood got a 1967 model Wienermobile out of storage and had a fiberglass mold made of it. This became the shell for the '88. Six molds were made and shipped to the Stevens brothers.

With the Stevenses beginning their work, Lovrien and her crew started planning the Wienermobile's coming-out party. It would be one of the biggest media events in Oscar Mayer's history—a national introduction to take place July 4, 1988, in New York's Central Park.

But in April 1988, Rick Wood realized that the new Wienermobiles were not going to be ready in time for the grand introduction. Unfortunately, it was too late for Oscar Mayer to change the New York event since media had been set up and permits had been granted.

Lovrien was emphatic that the launch happen as planned. "I made my famous statement—it's not a matter of getting it done on time, it's a matter of how we get it done on time."

Lovrien and Wood went down to Mequon for a "soul search meeting" with Dave and Steve Stevens. Wood recalls, "They basically broke down and said, 'No, we can't do it. It's beyond our capability.' So I asked what they'd need to get them done. And they said, 'Help.'"

Help came in the form of Oscar Mayer's Machine Development Group. The division that built hot dog processing machines and bologna slicers was now tasked with a completely different job—assemble six Wienermobiles.

Ken Metham, Oscar Mayer's "garage guy," took a team to finish the project. It turned out to be a bigger job than anyone could have anticipated. The crew moved to Mequon full time and, according to Lovrien, "worked day and night and day and night to get that fleet completed. It's thanks to them we had the whole fleet."

"They built the Wienermobiles for us," says Rick Wood. "It was Oscar Mayer people that basically did it."

The Machine Development Group made a heroic effort, but only four of the six vehicles were ready for the New York launch . . . and even those weren't totally finished. "Some of them didn't have the interiors complete," remembers Russ. "The driver's seat was on a plywood box."

The inside of the '88 Wienermobile was state of the art, with a microwave, refrigerator, and a cell phone. "The cell phone box itself was as big as a suitcase and it was permanently mounted to the wall. In 1988, that was something," says Russ. "Of course, like the microwave and the refrigerator, it never really worked that well, but it was a good PR piece."

In addition to the latest technology, the '88 Wienermobile also had an interesting gimmick—it was the world's first car that smelled like a hot dog. According to Russ, the vehicles had "little steam generators that were wallpaper steamers and they had a vent in the side of the buns that emitted the smell of hot dogs. You put a few drops of this on a steamer and . . . well, that didn't really work either."

Despite the undercooked Wienermobiles, the New York launch attracted a lot of attention. "They had a kick-off party at Tavern on the Green and they had several NFL players there," says Whitacre. "They had clowns, and balloon tiers, and they brought in underprivileged kids and served hot dogs. It was a pretty big PR event for its day."

Lovrien recalls, "We got a satellite feed. At that time, satellites were brand new. We got the coverage available to two hundred cities, and about eighty picked it up and showed it."

After New York, the Wienermobiles were sent back to Mequon so the Machine Development Group could finish building them. Each vehicle ended up costing between $80,000 and $85,000.

Meanwhile, Oscar Mayer had already hired its first group of Hotdoggers. Now if only they had something to drive . . .

CHAPTER 31

Mardi Gras—an event so gigantic that it requires two Wiener-mobiles, five Hotdoggers, and one paid parade consultant. Over the next eleven days we'll participate in ten parades, distribute thousands of whistles, and use countless puns. Logistically, I can only compare it to landing a man on the moon.

Sofia and I got into town last night after one hell of a long drive. We left Orlando at 11 a.m. and pulled into New Orleans twelve hours later. I drove about seven of those hours since Sofia was "so tired." She even wanted to stop and sleep in Mobile, a scant two hours from our goal. I said that wasn't a good idea.

"Fine, then you drive the rest of the way," she said. And so I did while she slept in the back. Even worse, once we arrived she took our shared laptop for the night, depriving me of both e-mail and my beloved Sim City game. Somehow that girl always wins.

But all is forgiven in the fresh light of a New Orleans morning. Joining Sofia and me on this grand adventure into the heart of drunken darkness is the relatively new team of Melissa and Luke. We last saw them right before Thanksgiving, when seven Hotdoggers decided it would be a good idea to cram into one hotel room in Chicago. It wasn't a good idea.

Melissa and Luke seem like they'd make a terrible team. Melissa is loud, outgoing, and often inappropriate; Luke is quiet, calm, and clean cut. Melissa is a world traveler; Luke had never been on a plane until last year. Melissa enjoys a few drinks; Luke is strictly sober. Yet despite their differences, these two have become the best of friends. Once again, the Wienermobile Department has put together a winning combination.

To further help the cause, headquarters has also flown in our old partner Ali. Poor Ali. Like many girls I know, her life has been in a downward spiral since we broke up. Ali was reassigned to Madison with the promise that she'd help out around the office for a few weeks and then be put on another team. Days turned into weeks turned into months. Apparently Ali so brightened the drab Oscar Mayer offices that they dropped plans to relocate her. The last few months have seen her staying at the Madison Residence Inn as an actual resident. She drives a rental car to work, knows the receptionist's first name, and generally lives a very stable nine-to-five existence. Everything she'd hoped to escape is now hers.

Our new super team has an appointment at Copeland's, a New Orleans chain started by the founder of Popeye's Fried Chicken. We're meeting with Jeff, a parade consultant and veteran of many a Mardi Gras. Jeff will be our guardian angel in New Orleans.

We find Jeff sitting alone at a large, round table. He has thinning black hair, meticulously combed over for maximum coverage. He's a surprisingly fragile fellow who doesn't look like he was raised on red beans and rice. Jeff stands to shake our hands, and I'm careful not to grip too hard for fear of crushing bone into powder. I notice his crisp brown pants. They were probably bought a few decades ago, most likely during JC Penney's Bicentennial Sale. This man should be tuning pianos, safely away from the spirited celebration of Mardi Gras. But, as Jeff quickly points out, we're not here to party. We're here to parade.

The drunken crowds on Bourbon Street get most of the attention, but parades are really the highlight of Carnival season. They are put on by organizations known as krewes, whose members pay an annual fee, ranging from $20 to several thousand dollars, for the privilege of participating in the parades and tossing beads to the masses. Some of the more exclusive krewes hire professional float builders, while the smaller groups have their members build their floats. Krewes then select a king or queen from within their ranks to reign over the festivities.

But krewes don't let just anyone into their parades. It's a very political process, and you need a local voice trumpeting your cause. That's where Jeff comes in. He's paid to get us into the game.

After lunch, Jeff takes us to his car (also from 1976) and pulls two large cardboard posters out of his trunk. One is a mask of comedy, the other of tragedy. "You'll need these," he says.

Jeff explains that we need to cover the Oscar Mayer rhomboids on the back of the Wienermobile. Mardi Gras, being above all a serious religious tradition, doesn't permit commercialization. Girls taking off their tops are fine, but no one can know who owns the giant hot dogs. Logically, it seems silly to think that taping up these masks will make anonymous the world's most un-anonymous car. But maybe a few people will be fooled into thinking we're an andouille sausage.

The other commercial concession involves the Wiener Whistles, those tiny trinkets we'll be tossing to lucky parade watchers. To meet with the event's commercialization ban, headquarters has shipped us sanitized whistles. Gone is the Oscar Mayer sticker—replaced with a generic "Mardi Party" logo that was obviously designed by some species of monkey. Worse yet, most of the stickers refuse to stick. Or, if they do stick, they stick to each other, creating a messy Mardi Party ball. This is how Oscar Mayer sends us off to war.

With two Wienermobiles in town, we decide to split up the parades and mix up the teams. It's Mardi Gras—might as well go nuts.

By some stroke of luck or fate or karma, Ali and I are reunited for the Bard's Parade, which takes place on the west side of New Orleans. But where on the west side? We have no idea because Jeff, the expert local, has given us wrong directions. Not just wrong directions, but crazy-wrong directions. Some of the turns he suggests are illegal; others are just impossible.

"I think you need to make a left up there," I tell Ali.

"No, that will just take us back on the highway."

"If you say so."

Arguing with Ali . . . I have missed these moments.

The parade is scheduled to start at 7 p.m. It's now eight. The first four people we ask for directions are useless. With no map, we're forced to drive around aimlessly for another hour through neighborhoods that don't see many tourists, let alone giant hot dogs.

Eventually, we see streetlights ahead. "Go toward the light! Go toward the light!" I shout.

We've found the parade. Unfortunately, we're two hours late. The flustered organizers emerge from shadows looking less than happy. Add torches and you'd have a scene from *Frankenstein*.

They all yell at once:

"You were supposed to be here at 7!"

"We had you guys at the front of the parade!"

"Do you realize how late you are?"

"Are you crazy?!"

The queen bee marches up and knocks on the window. "Pull up in front of that last float over there," she says. "And get ready to go."

"Yes, ma'am. Right away."

Ali and I spend a few minutes perfecting our parade routine. Normally we'd just sit and wave, but Mardi Gras crowds demand more . . . much more.

Our system goes like this. Ali will crawl out the bunroof and sit on top of the Wienermobile. To make sure she doesn't fall off, the company has supplied a safety belt. It looks like something you'd wear mountain climbing. Safely strapped in, Ali will then toss whistles to the masses. We've been given only a few boxes of Mardi Party whistles, however, so there's pressure to be frugal with them. I'm sure the people will understand.

While Ali's up top, I'll keep the Wienermobile at a slow, steady speed and try to avoid swerving into the crowd. Then we'll swap jobs after an hour. It's the perfect plan.

At 9:30 p.m., we're finally flagged forward. The first ten minutes are quiet as we drive through the now-deserted staging area. But the silence doesn't last long. I veer right, following a long, lazy curve. Rounding the bend, it's as if someone cranked the volume from 1 to 11. Suddenly we're parting a sea of outstretched arms. I can make out very few faces, but hands are everywhere. And those hands are up close, coming within inches of the bun. My own hands grip the steering wheel tighter as I see there's not much room for error here.

"BEADS! WE WANT BEADS! GIVE US SOME BEADS!"

The crowd is loud and insistent. Sometimes you can pick out an individual yell.

"HEY! WIENER LADY! THROW ME SOMETHING!"

"I WANT A BEAD, PRETTY LADY!"

"Toss some whistles!" I yell up to Ali.

"I'm waiting!" she yells back.

"Waiting for what?! Just throw them!"

Ali heaves a handful of whistles. Instead of having a calming effect, the whistles ignite some primal fury in the crowd. Having been fed a steady diet of beads, they are hungry for something different.

"Dave! I need more whistles!" soon comes the call from above.

I put the Wienermobile in park and rush to the back, ripping open a box of whistles from the supply closet. I dump the contents in our canvas bag and hand it up to Ali. A few seconds up there without whistles must feel like an eternity.

At 11 p.m. we're only halfway done with the parade. We've traveled about three miles and now it's my time on the roof. I somehow hoist my ample frame, nicely plumped from days of saturated Cajun cuisine, through the small opening. The view from up top is incredible—a sea of people in every direction. Some wear elaborate costumes, while others look like they've slept on the street. Every race, creed, and color is represented in this massive menagerie.

"HEY, WIENIE DUDE! WHERE'S MY WHISTLE AT?!"

If only the people weren't so obnoxious.

I belt myself in and cautiously start tossing. As scary as it was driving through this horde, at least I was protected by the Wienermobile's thick fiberglass skin. Now I'm out in the open, completely vulnerable. Whenever we come to a stop, the crowd surges against the interlocking metal barriers. Someone grabs for my shoe. Another person sails a water bottle just over my head. The whistles become my ammunition, my only defense against the throng. I grab and throw, grab and throw, grab and throw . . .

The citizens of New Orleans are nothing if not resourceful. Hell, they built their city below sea level. And they'll go to even greater lengths to get a whistle. Some people employ nets on long aluminum poles or handmade lifeguard chairs to gain some height. One man uses his daughter as a fishing pole. "HEY! GIVE MY KID A WHISTLE!" he says as the young lady is dangled near my shoes. For her, I don't toss. I simply hand over the loot. She smiles as she's slowly retracted back and swallowed by the mob.

Bribes are offered. "FIVE BUCKS FOR A WHISTLE!" screams a voice from below.

It starts to drizzle around midnight, but I seem to be the only one who notices. The crowd stays strong, fueled by alcohol and the promise of free plastic.

The end comes unceremoniously and unexpectedly. We turn a corner and suddenly everything just opens up. The tightly packed people are gone, replaced by lone walkers, sadly dragging empty coolers or folding lawn chairs. Deprived of the group's collective will and energy, these stragglers only have the strength to raise an eyebrow as we pass.

"Whistle? Can I get a whistle?" they whisper in hoarse voices.

I climb down from the crow's nest, happy to still have my health, my sanity, and my shoes.

Finally, we all have a night off in New Orleans and the goal is clear—drink heartily from the Mardi Gras cup. Our merry band of travelers (Luke, Sofia, Melissa, Ali, myself, and assorted friends) plan to wear the beads, fight the crowds, and see the breasts. This is why people come to the Crescent City, to get so drunk that they can't remember where they are.

Tonight we have a special guest—Atlanta Ashley. She's in town to visit Sofia and to experience Mardi Gras for the first time. And while part of me is looking forward to reconnecting, another part wants to run and hide. I'm sure I'll have the opportunity to do both.

Since there are no affordable hotels in New Orleans proper, we've been staying at the Residence Inn in Metairie, about fifteen miles from all the action. The hotel is nice, but the location is not ideal. We can expense only $20 a week in cab fares, and around here that will barely get you out of the parking lot. But since we can expense gas, someone came up with the ingenious solution of bartering for cab rides. As in, "we'll fill up your cab with super unleaded and you give us a free ride." It works like a charm.

At nine o'clock, a cab drops us off a few blocks from Bourbon Street.

"Good luck," says the cab driver. "And thanks for the gas!"

Stepping out of the cab, there's no need to ask for directions. We just follow the cheerful cacophony, through alleys and around road-blocks, until at last we're deposited on Bourbon Street. I know we've made it when I spot a guy throwing up into a sewer grate.

"Who's ready to party?" asks Ashley as she takes the first brave step toward the crowd.

The crowd at Mardi Gras is not some peaceful assemblage of strangers. No, the crowd at Mardi Gras is a force of nature. Like the ocean current, it controls where you go and how fast you get there.

Forget what people tell you about Mardi Gras. It's not a casual, laid-back good time. It's not even a good time. It's more like the running of the bulls. Except everyone's a bull, and so you're running from yourself. Which all makes a lot more sense after you've had seven hurricanes and something called a grenade.

After an hour of bouncing from bar to bar, my head is light and my vision hazy. While the rest of our crew stops to refill, Ashley grabs me by the arm and wordlessly leads me outside. Perhaps alcohol has switched off her normally prudent judgment; perhaps I'm finally going to get that kiss.

"I need to find a bathroom," she says. Well, at least it's together time.

Here's another thing they don't tell you in the brochures—it's impossible to find a bathroom during Mardi Gras. There are no public toilets and the bars all charge money for the privilege. That's right— there's a cover charge for the bathrooms, sometimes as high as $10. Ashley's a television producer; she can afford to pee. But I have principles and a miniscule paycheck. Besides, you shouldn't have to pay for something that's free the other 364 days of the year. So I leave Ashley in a long bathroom line and begin my slow stagger around the area, looking for a place to mark my territory.

The urge to go quickly balloons into a painful problem. It feels like someone stuck a dagger in my side and is poking my angry bladder. A few more seconds of this and I'm going to have a different problem.

Then I spot salvation in front of a nearby church. The location is perfect—it's dark, desolate, and there's already a vagrant peeing on the front steps. I feel like God put this church here specifically so that I could relieve myself.

I walk to the church just as quickly as my hunched posture will allow and pick a spot next to my new best friend, a haggard man who spent more time braiding his beard than washing it. He looks over, somewhat surprised to have company.

"How's it going?" I ask, trying to maintain an air of civility.

"Mmmmhhhmmm," is his response. I couldn't agree more.

I unzip and get to business. The relief is immense, instant, and the greatest sensation I can remember. My posture improves incrementally and soon I'm standing tall, proudly claiming these steps for all those in need of a free pee. In my alcohol-battered brain, this is my finest moment.

And then a voice, loud and firm, interrupts my triumph. "HEY! TURN AROUND!"

Startled, I quickly tuck in, turn my head, and find myself staring at a horse's head. I know I'm drunk, but this seems like a strange hallucination.

My unbelieving eyes slowly drift upward and there I find the source of the sound: a mounted police officer. He looks to be one hundred feet tall and is none too happy.

"What do you think you're doing?" asks the giant.

A thousand answers rush through my mind, none of them the truth and few of them even probable. Before I can answer, instinct takes over.

I run. I run hard down a dark side street.

Just a few seconds into my sprint, instinct gives way to panic. *I'm running from a mounted cop! Why am I running from a mounted cop?!*

Panic soon turns to regret. *I really shouldn't be running from a mounted cop!*

But I'm too far down the fugitive path now. I seek refuge in a small, corner bar. It's a walk-up joint, meaning there are no doors, just folded-back windows. Great if you're looking to get in quickly, not so great if you're looking to hide from the law.

My arrival causes a good deal of commotion, as I'm now being followed by two cops on horseback. I guess Cop Number 1 called for backup. My eyes dart around and I see that there's no way out. Escape is impossible. Defeated, I walk outside with my head down and my hands up. Just like they do in the movies.

I'm immediately met by the officer who first found me. He expertly leaps off his horse and swats down my arms. "Boy, that was a stupid thing to do," he says, shoving me hard against a brick wall. My arms are jerked behind my back and the handcuffs tightly applied. "Come on, let's go."

The officer parades me down Bourbon. "I was just going to give you a warning," he says. "But then you had to run. Ha!"

My eyes are firmly fixed on wet asphalt. But there are hundreds of eyes firmly fixed on me. I've become the twisted car crash that everyone slows down to see.

And then, my darkest hour gets just a bit dimmer.

"Dave?"

I look over and see . . . who else? Ashley. She's coming out of the bathroom, having happily spent $10 to avoid handcuffs. There's a look of sheer shock on her face as she comes running over. "What happened?" she asks.

"I peed on a church."

"You what?! Where are they taking you?"

"To jail. Tell Sofia and Melissa."

Ashley watches as they put me in the back of a paddy wagon. Looking at her sad, disappointed face makes me realize just how much I lost tonight. The heavy doors of the paddy wagon are unceremoniously shut. My incarceration has officially begun. Through a grated window, I watch the crowd swallow Ashley up.

My new surroundings are small and steel. A flattened Yankees cap lies pathetically on the floor, providing the only touch of ambiance. I sit on the cold bench and lean back, my handcuffs clanging against the metal wall. The thought suddenly occurs—what if Sofia and Melissa decide to call Russ? This is the man who made me write a letter of apology after a speeding ticket. He finds out about this and I'm going to be the first Hotdogger ever fired for public urination. Try explaining that to the parents or my second grade math teacher.

After fifteen minutes alone in the truck, I realize two things: (1) these officers are in no hurry, and (2) I still have to go to the bathroom.

The horse interrupted me in mid-stream, so my bladder is still quite full. An arrest might sober you up, but it has absolutely no effect on the urinary system. I look around in despair, but there are no facilities in the back of the wagon. I think about screaming for help, but decide not to test my officer's patience again.

Minutes pass and the pain grows. By now, it's that old, familiar feeling. My only option, besides drenching these new jeans, is the discarded baseball hat. Being a Cubs fan, I have no moral objection to peeing on a Yankees hat, but there are a few logistical difficulties. First is the fact that my arms are handcuffed behind my back. Also, there's precious little privacy in the paddy wagon. Who knows when they'll fling open the doors and toss in a roommate.

The need to urinate might be the strongest human motivator—stronger than hunger, money, and sex combined. Having already turned criminal, I know that it does strange things to a man. I try to be rational, but it's no use. The bladder wins again.

I kneel on the cold metal floor and waddle forward until I'm positioned over the baseball hat. After some Houdini-esque contortions, my fly comes down and the peeing begins in earnest. Only now, the thrill of release is gone, replaced with an overwhelming fear of being caught.

Thankfully, the doors remain shut and I'm able to finish my business. Now I've just got to hope that no one wants to wear this hat.

After another hour of waiting, I'm finally driven to the jail and escorted out of the wagon. Once inside, I'm fingerprinted and photographed, and then taken to my new home—an ultra-bright holding cell. Unlike the lonely paddy wagon, I've got plenty of company now. I count fifteen of us in an enclosure not much bigger than a McDonald's bathroom. And like a McDonald's bathroom, there's a toilet in the corner. Ironically, I no longer need to go.

My cellmates include every cliché criminal imaginable, from the bandana-wearing biker to the mumbling psychopath to the man with the tattooed face. With my khaki pants and collared shirt, I'm way overdressed for such an informal gathering.

Mardi Gras is not a good time to commit a crime in New Orleans. The cops are overworked and short on good humor. They could care less about our "rights" or the "Constitution." So while my cellmates continue to yell and scream, I slink to the back of the cell and pray that this nightmare will end soon.

"Come on, buddy," spits one of the guards in my general direction. "Time to use the phone."

My turn to make a collect call comes around 2 a.m. I have no idea who to call. Partners? They don't have cell phones. Parents? No need ruining their image of the perfect son. Friends in New Orleans? Don't have any. My only option is to call the hotel and ask to be connected to somebody's room. This jail doesn't offer much in the way of modern conveniences, but they do have a ratty copy of the Yellow Pages. It's chained to the wall, as if theft is a huge problem in here.

I dial the Metarie Residence Inn and am soon connected to the sleepy front desk. Before I can say anything, a recorded message comes on.

"This is a collect call from the New Orleans Penitentiary System. Would you like to accept a call from . . ."

So much for discretion. "Dave Ihlenfeld. I'm with the Wienermobile. I need to talk to my partner. Please pick up. Please . . ."

The confused clerk takes pity and accepts the call. She puts me through to Melissa's room.

"Hello?" she answers in a groggy, alcohol-laced voice.

"Melissa, it's Dave. I'm in jail."

"Dave! We tried calling, but—"

"You didn't call Russ, did you?!"

Melissa pauses on the other line. "Why would we call Russ?"

Good question. Seems my paddy wagon worrying was for nothing.

I hurry to explain my situation, telling Melissa that I can post bond in the morning and that there's no need to worry.

"Okay," she responds. Doesn't seem like she was worrying. "Just be careful in there."

I hang up and am promptly escorted back to my cell.

As the night goes on, the air grows heavy and I wear it like a lead blanket. The florescent lights never blink, painting everything an eerie white. Sleep is impossible. My only rest comes from crouching in the corner.

At 7 a.m. comes the most melodic thing I've ever heard. "Ihlenfeld! David!" yells one of the guards. "Let's go!" I leave my corner and walk toward that beautiful voice.

Bond is $500. Fortunately there's an ATM four inches from the booking desk. Minutes later I'm outside, staring at a real sky and huffing that moist New Orleans air. I run down the street with my arms flapping like a bird. I must look like a real jackass, but I don't care.

The next day I appear in court and reunite with all my cellmate buddies. Even though we went through quite an ordeal together, no one says much. I doubt we'll be exchanging Christmas cards this year.

The judge moves everyone through with a sort of heartless efficiency. My name gets called and I step up to the podium. "How do you plead?" asks the judge.

"No contest, your honor." It sounds better than "guilty."

My punishment is a $300 fine, which I gladly pay to get some closure on my night of a thousand mistakes.

What happened to Ashley? She left before I got back to the hotel. Not that it matters. What do you say to a girl after she's seen you in handcuffs?

My partners offer nothing but support and sympathy. After an initial barrage of questions, they graciously stop talking about the incident. Life on the road goes on.

The next day is a drive day as Sofia and I head back to Florida.

"I'll drive," she offers in the morning.

"Thanks."

The drive is long and the route is familiar, leaving me with a lot of time to obsess about my night in the slammer. *Why am I such a screw-up? What am I doing with my life?* I can be pretty hard on myself, but the weight of failure has never felt so heavy.

I'm twenty-two years old and, in many respects, still a child. I shun adult responsibilities, adult decisions, adult obligations. I took this job not because it was a coveted opportunity, but because it offered the promise of prolonging puberty. Might be time to grow up, Dave.

A few hours into the trip, Sofia mercifully breaks the silence. "You doing okay, Davey?"

"Yeah. I guess."

"It's not that big of a deal. Only a few people know about it."

"I just feel so stupid."

"Don't feel stupid. It's not your fault."

I turn to look at sweet Sofia, who immediately realizes her mistake. "Well, I guess it's kind of your fault," she says, trying hard to contain a chuckle.

For the first time in two days, I smile.

CHAPTER 32

Hotdoggers I were a ragtag group who had no idea what they were getting into. Then again, Oscar Mayer didn't know what they were getting into either. After ten years in hibernation, the Wienermobile was again ready to roll.

According to Russ Whitacre, the first Hotdoggers hired were mostly "sons and daughters of friends and relatives." They came from schools that Oscar Mayer would continue to recruit from over the years—Penn State, Texas, Wisconsin. The inaugural group went through a week of training, dubbed Hot Dog High by Phyllis Lovrien. Training was basic at first. "We didn't have much driver training, certainly didn't have any diversity training," remembers Russ. "We didn't do as much team building. It was pretty much come in, sit down in a classroom, here are some things to help the company, here's what your job's going to be, here's how to fill out an expense report, and here are the keys."

After Hot Dog High, the fresh hires sat around and waited for the Wienermobiles to be finished. In late August 1988, they were finally ready. Now, Oscar Mayer had to figure out what to do with their new toys.

"Back then, we really didn't even know what we were doing," says Rick Wood. "It was what we used to call guerilla marketing. You just go *into a city and do it. Call a chamber. Back then we were allowed to go to schools. Call a school, call an older folks center, and just show up."*

According to a first-year Hotdogger, *"They didn't give us anything to do. There was no real sense of what the program was."* According to the Hotdogger the Wienermobile was *"more just a novelty at that point."*

But soon, the Wienermobile would find its role. Hotdoggers began hitting retail stores with the goal of re-establishing the Wienermobile in the minds of consumers. The plan seemed to be working.

"In 1987, the awareness of the Wienermobile was 44 percent. Probably as many people knew about Little Oscar as they did the Wienermobile," says Russ. *"By 1996 or so, it was like 90 percent. And that was pretty much with unpaid advertising and exposure."*

While the Wienermobile was turning heads on the road, things weren't so sunny at Oscar Mayer headquarters. Phyllis Lovrien, who had spearheaded the Wienermobile revival, left in 2003. Oscar Mayer turned to a woman from inside the company with a background in product publicity. She may have had the experience, but, according to Russ, *"she wasn't into the nuts and bolts of it, wasn't into answering the phone at midnight and dealing with all the personnel issues."*

When it came time to make a change, Russ raised his hand. *"It was sort of a dicey thing to replace her, but I had a good relationship with the Hotdoggers. I spent a lot of time out traveling with them, I spent a lot of time talking to them that she wouldn't, so to me it was a great opportunity to get involved in it."*

Russ became the head of the Wienermobile Department in 1990. His first order of business was to deal with the problem of unreliable vehicles. The '88 Wienermobiles looked nifty, but they were proving to be mechanical nightmares.

"From the get-go, they always overheated," says transportation manager Rick Wood. *"They always had electrical problems. Within a couple of years, we were starting to replace engines and transmissions. It was a mess."*

Wood wasn't the only one who didn't have a lot of faith in the '88s.

"There wasn't a lot of thought placed on the engineering and the design of it," says Russ. "It was 'Okay, let's build Wienermobiles.' They ended up with something that was uncomfortable and impossible to air-condition."

Each '88 was averaging around forty thousand miles a year, and the cost of maintenance kept rising. As soon as he took charge, Russ began plotting the next generation of Wienermobiles. "I wanted to have vehicles that could stay on the road, drive down the road, be repaired, and keep on going," he says. "It was a good job. I didn't want to lose it."

Russ began researching different automotive designers. That's when he came across the name Harry Bentley Bradley.

Bradley was an automotive design instructor at the Art Center College of Design in Pasadena who had a long career in the auto industry. In 1962, he started working for the General Motors design staff. In 1968, Bradley designed eleven of the original sixteen Hot Wheels cars. He also designed the Chevrolet El Camino.

Russ and Rick Wood met with Bradley at his home in Palos Verdes, California, to explain their goals for the new vehicles. "Mechanically, we wanted it to operate a lot better," says Wood. "We wanted it to show more pizzazz and be more open. We wanted to use the vehicle as more of a marketing tool."

Bradley jumped at the opportunity to upgrade an automotive icon and quickly made some sketches. "Harry would go through and draw up some designs," remembers Russ. "Some of them were very outlandish—he had side pipes and portholes. On some of them, he had an exterior panel that would slide out and there was going to be a big screen TV in there."

Bradley also toyed with other notions: a six-pack of wieners, a hot dog 4x4, and a convertible wiener. Eventually he struck upon a design that both referenced the past and looked ahead to the future.

CHAPTER 33

S o," starts Russ as he marches around a rustic conference room, "Let's talk about the future."

Uh-oh. He wants to talk about the future.

All the Hotdoggers have been gathered together in the resort town of Green Lake, Wisconsin. This is not a very exciting place to be in mid-March. In fact, I think that our group is the only thing keeping this hotel open. I can only imagine the amazing group rate that Russ was able to score.

Life on the road has been rough since the Mardi Gras incident. I feel emotionally dirty every time I flash back to my night in jail. That's no place for a Phi Beta Kappa. I also feel like I let everyone down, which is a bit silly since only a few people know about the incident.

To repent, I've decided to become a better Hotdogger. I pass out more whistles, push more product, and no longer rush through conversations with customers. If someone wants to talk about the evolution of Wienermobile chassis, I'm now happy to oblige.

One day, Sofia noticed my strange behavior. "Are you feeling all right?" she asked.

"Feeling great! Just trying to spread some smiles."

Sofia could only glare at me, supreme suspicion in her eyes. "No, really. Are you sick or something?"

With only three months left in our Hotdogger careers, we were all curious about the point of this spring summit. Couldn't headquarters just send out a memo instead of flying in every team? But now the purpose seems obvious—Russ wants to prepare us for life after the Wienermobile. It's time to start looking forward instead of checking the rearview mirror.

Russ starts the torture by highlighting the myriad jobs that Hotdoggers have gone on to do. "There's Pat, who's a speech language pathologist in Tampa. Isabella, an attorney with the U.S. Postal Service in Chicago. Mark, an immigration inspector in Hawaii. Kevin, director of cheese marketing in Rosemont..."

And the list goes on. Some ex-Hotdoggers went back to school, some went to work for Kraft, others took time off and traveled the world. So, basically, this job prepares you for everything and nothing at the same time.

"At the end of the year you'll get a list of all the former Hotdoggers—their names, their address and e-mails, and what they do for a living," says Russ. "Call these people, seek out their advice, and find out if they can help you."

They'd better be able to help me.

Russ continues his presentation. "Okay, we're going to go around the room and everyone can talk about what they're planning to do after the Wienermobile."

The conversation slowly winds around the table, each Hotdogger bravely baring their respective hopes and ambitions. Most of the plans are vague—Melissa might work in sports marketing, Ali wants to star on Broadway. Sofia dreams of moving to LA. Only a few people know for certain. Luke will be returning to William and Mary to get his master's in education. Jamila is going to the University of Virginia for a masters in, of all things, neuroscience. Ben will be working at a service-oriented summer program for high school students on a Montana Indian reservation.

But I have no grad school or hippie summer camp in my future, so I keep revising and rehearsing an answer in my head, desperately trying to spin gold out of complete bull.

"David, what do you have planned?" asks Russ when it's my turn under the hot light.

"Well, I think I'm going to live in my parents' basement. Probably only come up for meals and holidays."

"But seriously . . ." prompts Russ.

Gulp. "Actually, I don't know what I want to do."

"That's okay. Do you know what you *don't* want to do?"

I'm momentarily stunned by Russ's Zen-like question. "I hadn't really thought of it that way. I don't want a desk job, something that's just nine to five. I want to keep traveling. I want to find something creative to do."

"Sounds like a promising start," says Russ.

After the meeting, I slink out of the room, anxious to be alone with my thoughts. But there's no such thing as alone time when you're among a group of Hotdoggers. Melissa catches up to me in the hallway. "I liked the part about living in your parents' basement."

"Thanks. Hey, aren't you worried about what comes after this?"

"Not really. I know I want to move to Chicago."

"And do what?"

"I'm not sure, but I'll figure it out."

"You sound pretty confident."

"It's not that big of a deal. Don't you remember in one of those Wienermobile videos they showed us? There were all these people who had really great jobs who had been Hotdoggers."

"Um . . . I don't remember that."

"All I know is I'm gonna use this so well on my resume that people will want to hire me right away."

I later ask Russ if transitioning to life outside the bun is a common problem among Hotdoggers. "One of the things we've noticed is that there are different groups of people," he says. "Some people need to have a job as soon as they finish. If they don't have a job to start with the next week, they are just going crazy. They feel they need to make the transition very quickly. Some of them make some dumb mistakes in terms of where they go, for example, jumping into a sales job where someone paints them a great picture with a lot of commission, and it's really a lot of cold calling. So there is a lot of reality check of, 'I don't want to do that.' Some people just want to chill for a while and travel. And that's cool. I envy them."

Russ tells the story of a former employee who took the road less traveled, a young woman who was a Hotdogger and then an advisor for a year. Her parents wanted her to come home and put that good University of Missouri training to use, get a job, and settle down. She had the opportunity to go to Europe and asked for Russ's advice. Russ said, "Martha, I wouldn't tell many people this, but don't listen to your parents. Go to Europe." She did, and she ended up on a cruise ship, where she met her husband. She changed her life by doing that.

But for every happy tale about love and a life fulfilled, there's a sad story about Hotdoggers who dreaded the end of the road. There are tales about Hotdoggers who, at the end of the run, had nothing else they wanted to or could do. They return to real life, get some menial job, and have trouble adjusting. Some former Hotdoggers report feeling the shock of completely anonymous again, and having to actively break themselves of the habit of waving to people.

It seems like life after the Wienermobile is black or white: love on a cruise ship or misery in a minimum-wage job. Either way, Green Lake is a wake-up call, a bucket of cold water, a kick in the teeth, a slap in the face.

The future is going to happen. Best get ready for it.

Besides marking the beginning of the end for our Hotdogger

careers, Green Lake is the end of the end for my partnership with Sofia. Proving that everything comes full circle with the Wienermobile, she'll be reuniting with Ali on a tour of yet more grocery stores while I jet off to Europe.

Sofia and I had plenty of good times and never any bad ones. She's funny, personable, and still easy on the eyes. Our relationship has evolved quite a lot in the past ten months. We've gone from strangers to great friends. Personally, I've gone from lust to love. But more the kind you'd feel for a sister than the "let's have sex in the Wienermobile" variety.

That's not to say I didn't give it one last try. On Valentine's Day, as we were driving down yet another bleak interstate, I turned and caught her eye.

"What?" she said.

"Let's have sex and never talk about it."

She looked at me blankly for a second and then burst out laughing. To this day, we still laugh about that joke.

Thing is, I wasn't joking.

CHAPTER 34

R uss Whitacre and Rick Wood spent almost a year in close collaboration with automotive designer Harry Bentley Bradley and eventually settled on a Wienermobile blueprint everyone was happy with. The next step was getting management to sign off.

Alas, the approval process was happening during a tumultuous period for Oscar Mayer. The company had been bought by General Foods in 1981. Four years later, General Foods was bought by Philip Morris, which also owned Kraft at the time. In 1988, Philip Morris merged Kraft and General Foods into Kraft General. Oscar Mayer now fell under the rather large Kraft umbrella.

"It was a tough time at Oscar Mayer," says Russ. "There were some cutbacks. It was transitioning from sort of an independent company to being more of a Kraft company. It had gone through being owned by Philip Morris and General Foods, and they had never influenced it much. It was pretty much still a stand-alone organization, but as Kraft started to get more involved in it, there started to be more management, more approvals, and everything else."

Russ was asking for in excess of $1 million to build six new Wienermobiles, and the company was hesitant to commit so much money. But

Kraft executives, recognizing the value of this unique marketing strategy, eventually did sign off on the project. Prototype Source, a concept car company based in Pasadena, constructed a scale model of the new Wienermobile and even tested it in the wind tunnel at Cal Tech. A plywood mock-up was then built on a full-scale chassis to test the steering system and driver placement.

Next came the tough part: finding someone to actually build the Wienermobile. At the time, there were very few companies doing that kind of work. Oscar Mayer came close to signing with a manufacturer of motorized trolley cars before Russ was contacted by a man named Kevin Carlin. Russ recalls Carlin telling him, "I know what you want. I know what a Wienermobile is, I grew up with them. This is something I want to do."

Carlin owned a company in Fresno, California, called, conveniently enough, Carlin Manufacturing. During the first Gulf War, the government contracted Carlin to make hundreds of military kitchens for soldiers in the Middle East. Now Carlin wanted to enter an entirely different field of combat: mobile marketing.

"We went out to Fresno," says Russ. "They hadn't done too much in specialty work, but they put together a bid and it looked pretty good. So we thought, 'Let's go with these guys.'"

It was decided that the new Wienermobiles would be built on GMC Dually truck chassis. Starting in the summer of 1994, the bodies were molded and sculpted by Carlin and then shipped down to the tiny desert town of Adelanto, California, where the same company that had built the original Corvette body did the fiberglass work. The fiberglass parts were then shipped back to Carlin and assembled on the chassis.

The pieces were coming together, but nobody anticipated the engineering challenges of creating a twenty-seven-foot designer hot dog. "One of the greatest challenges was the doors," says Russ. "The doors were too heavy. There was an external key and that would turn on a hydraulic loader and that would pump hydraulic fluid to the cylinders and that would open the door. It was very spaceship-ish. Sometimes they

didn't always work, though. If you lost power, you'd be stuck inside or out."
The builders also needed to add secondary generators in the trunk to run
the air-conditioning and other electrical systems.

While the manufacturing was going on, Kevin Carlin sold his business and moved to New Zealand. With Carlin gone, the Wienermobile
project ran into manufacturing problems and cost overruns. Oscar
Mayer eventually had to pony up more money to keep the project moving
forward.

The Wienermobiles still weren't finished for the extravagant media
launch, exactly the same thing that happened with the introduction of the
'88s. Only three '95s were available for the February 1 event, which was
held in an airplane hangar in Los Angeles. The dogs looked good on the
outside, but the interiors had yet to be completed.

Work continued on the Wienermobiles even as another deadline
loomed: the July 1 launch of Talent Search, Oscar Mayer's promotional
campaign to find a child star for one of its commercials. The last '95
Wienermobile was completed just two days before an inaugural Talent
Search event in Oklahoma City. Russ, along with two Hotdoggers, picked
up the vehicle in Fresno and drove six and a half hours to Kingman,
Arizona. The next day, they traveled more than a thousand miles through
Arizona, New Mexico, Texas, and Oklahoma before arriving at their destination in the early morning hours. The Wienermobile made its opening
curtain, but just barely.

With the completion of the six '95 vehicles (license plates: OURDOG,
HOTDOG, YUMMY, WEENR, BIGBUN, and OSCAR) and the continued service of
four '88 dogs, Oscar Mayer had ten Wienermobiles on the road—its largest fleet ever. The '88s even got a makeover to keep them running through
Talent Search. The engines were replaced and two seats were removed in
the back to create more space. Modifications were also made to the cool-
ing systems, although the overheating problem would never be solved.

Manning this impressive armada were thirty Hotdoggers, three to
each vehicle. It was the golden age of the Wienermobile.

CHAPTER 35

The road sign reads AUTOBAHN—2 KM.

I'm not sure what that equates to in miles, but it can't be very far. Two, after all, is universally recognized as a small number. It's time to prepare for my greatest Hot-dogging challenge—conquering the German autobahn in an imported sausage.

My new partner Debbie and I arrived in Germany yesterday and are still a bit groggy from twelve hours crammed into coach. After an evening in the picture postcard city of Wurzburg, we picked up BIGBUN this afternoon from an importing warehouse. The Wienermobile looked comically out of place among a cluttered yard of tires, plants, and scrap metal. While BIGBUN survived the overseas journey, its battery did not. We had to commandeer a nearby forklift for an emergency jump start.

This six-week European excursion promises a host of interesting challenges. There's the language barrier, the cultural barrier, the vehicular barrier, and, of course, the teammate barrier.

Debbie and I have never worked together. Actually, we never had a lengthy conversation until a few weeks ago. Our paths crossed at Hot Dog High, of course, but we never made much effort to bond.

Debbie is a tall, confident African American with an athletic build, somewhere between pole-vaulter and basketball center. She speaks in a deep voice that never needs repeating, and she's not afraid to share her opinion.

It's hard to get a read on Debbie. I don't feel the lust I felt for Sofia or the warm fuzzies I felt for Ali. With Debbie I feel . . . well, I don't know what I feel. Hopeful ambivalence, maybe? Anyway, we'll have six weeks to sort out our emotions.

Forgetting my personal hesitations, Debbie has already proven a valuable partner. She did most of planning for this adventure—putting together our schedule, contacting the sales reps, sending out press releases, and making sure that we had enough supplies to last us for the duration. I picked up a few maps.

The autobahn frightens me. It's the world's first high-speed road network and the proving ground for some of the finest automobiles ever built. When we found out about this trip, driving the autobahn was my only real hesitation. I pictured exotic death cars zooming past our pokey hot dog at obscene speeds. And now that we're approaching the beast, I can actually see those exotic death cars zooming across the horizon.

With sweaty hands on the wheel, I take us onto the short entrance ramp. The merge is just ahead, cars whizzing by in a bright rainbow blur. I step on the gas, hoping to wrestle loose some sort of acceleration. We'll never be a blur, but a top speed above 35 mph would be nice.

I check the side mirror approximately ninety times, suck a deep reserve of air into my lungs, and then turn the wheel ever so slightly to the left. Immediately, I hear a scream and then a sickening thump. Tires screech behind us. My head whips left, my eyes just catching a wobbly motorcycle fishtailing wildly next to the Wienermobile. I didn't know he was there. Oh god, I didn't know. The cyclist is flipped out of frame. More screeching, more sick screams.

Actually, none of that happened. We merge just fine.

I confidently turn to Debbie. "Well, we're on the autobahn."

Debbie briefly looks up from the map. "Great."

The autobahn is not the death trap I had imagined. There are some very quick cars, but at least people seem in control of them. The same can't be said of your typical American highway, where it's usually survival of the fastest.

"Let's see what this baby can do," I say to Debbie while pressing down hard on the gas. The speedometer slowly climbs—forty-five, fifty-five, sixty-five, seventy-five, eighty.

"We're doing eighty!" I say triumphantly. I've never gotten the Wienermobile close to such a terminal velocity. Smiling like I've just won the Daytona 500, I notice an elderly woman pull alongside in a vintage silver Audi. She looks over in shock, then leans into the steering wheel and begins howling like a circus monkey. Then she bolts past us and disappears around the bend.

I soon find out that doing eighty on the autobahn is not an impressive feat. Unfortunately, the governor on our engine makes it impossible to go any faster. You'd think Oscar Mayer could have taken that thing off for this trip. Maybe it would have helped us fit in a little better.

As it is, we stick out to an embarrassing degree. There's a lot of honking, but over here it's because we're blocking traffic. A few drivers slow to stare, but absolutely no one dares to wave.

"I don't think they like us," I tell Debbie.

"Nah, they just don't know us yet."

A few kilometers later, we get a chance to make a proper introduction when we have to fill up for the first time. This is another thing I've been dreading. It's hard enough to escape an American gas station unharmed. How will we survive a German one?

As feared, a crowd of curious gawkers forms even before we shut off the engine. They stand at a distance, unsure if it's safe to approach. I walk over to see if Debbie needs any help buying gas. Remarkably, she seems to have figured out which German gasoline to buy. It helps that our local contact gave us very explicit directions. "Don't accidentally buy diesel," he warned us. "You'll blow up."

While Debbie works the pump, I work the crowd. Before leaving Madison, Debbie had the foresight to print up hundreds of cards that explain the Wienermobile in German. Since we don't know the language, this figured to be easier than pointing and grunting. The cards give a brief history of "Das Wienermobil" (highlighting Oscar F. Mayer's German heritage), explain our current mission, and make it clear that we come in peace. They begin: "Das 'Wienermobil' ist ein Warenzeichen-Fahrzeug der Firma Oscar Mayer Foods . . ." and list such features as "Sitze in Hot-dog relish" and "Teppiche in Gewuerzfarben."

The cards are an immediate success. I hand them out and watch eager eyes soak up the inspirational, if slightly stilted, words. An elderly man, his weight carefully rested on a wooden walking stick, looks up from his card with newfound recognition. "Ahhh, the Wurst Wagon," he says. (Although it sounds more like "Vurst Vagon")

Now convinced that we mean them no harm, the gas station groupies approach BIGBUN for a closer inspection. The Wienermobile gets poked, prodded, and relentlessly photographed. We hand out Wiener Whistles to everyone. Once again, there is confusion over these plastic trinkets. Debbie patiently holds one up and demonstrates a short whistle. Soon the whole station is whistling.

Just as we're about to leave, I notice an older gentleman, watching us from an adjacent pump. His gaze is strong and steady, like a wrinkled surveillance camera. "What do you think?" I ask, not even sure if he speaks English.

"Very American," he says with a deep laugh. "Very American."

So far BIGBUN has been behaving—no breakdowns, no overheating, no windows falling off. Today, however, we arrived at our military base event and something very peculiar happened. I tried turning off the engine, but it wouldn't turn off. The key came out, but the Wienermobile stayed on.

"Uh, Debbie, I think we might have a problem."

"What's happening?"

"The engine won't shut off," I said, holding up the key for dramatic effect.

"Try turning off the heater," said a calm and cool Debbie.

"The heater? What'll that do?"

"Just try it."

And so I shut off the heater and, sure enough, the engine shut off. Very strange.

We're only a few events in and have already discovered that military bases have a language all their own. "One p.m." is "thirteen hundred," "Kmart" is "PX," and "grocery store" is "commissary." Things can get mighty confusing if you don't pay attention. And, as Hotdoggers, we're not used to paying attention.

Commissaries are the reason we're in Europe. So far, base visits have been very similar to our grocery store appearances. We show up, struggle to turn off the engine, and then spend the rest of the day pretending to be busy.

There are a few differences. At every stop we're joined by the local S&K sales rep. S&K is the company that handles Oscar Mayer commissary sales for most of Europe. In addition to bringing us over, they've also scheduled our events and booked our hotel rooms. This is one hands-on corporation.

It's the job of the S&K rep to push product, and most do so by offering generous free samples. Great idea, except Debbie and I must man the grill. This would never, *ever*, happen in the States. During the interview process, Russ specifically mentioned that we would not be "handling product." But the rules are different overseas, and so Debbie and I become quite adept at grilling Oscar Mayer all-beef hot dogs. We're also getting pretty good at eating them. I've probably consumed more hot dogs in the past three days than in the last three years.

In addition to our altered duties, we also get some different questions overseas. The most popular are:

"How did you get that thing over here?" *Boat.*

"What do the Germans think about it?" *They love it!*

"Does it float?" *Um . . . no.*

I'm guessing base life is fairly dull because the people who come to see the Wienermobile tend to stick around for a while. They'll walk around the vehicle, talk to us, peek inside, read our signage, have a hot dog, and then do the whole routine all over again.

A boy who looks about ten or eleven walks over in awe. "Wow. Where is this from? What state?"

"Utopia," I answer.

"Dave! You're evil," chides Debbie.

On base, BIGBUN provides some educational opportunities. Teachers empty their classrooms, expecting us to have a Wienermobile lesson plan prepared. Drawing upon my natural ability to put one over kids, I usually give a brief lecture on the history of the Wienermobile and then let Debbie handle the guided tour. We've had to kick out only a few kids for excessive horn honking.

We've also developed something of a comedy routine. Debbie asks the kids a question, like "How many hot dogs does the Wienermobile weigh?" and while they're feverishly guessing, I sneak behind Debbie and hold up a sign with the correct answer. It's not Jim Carrey, but the kids love it.

We're very popular with the military crowds. It's a nice change from the often-indifferent Walmart patrons. On base, the Wienermobile is accorded the American icon status it deserves:

"Thank you so much for being here. This is great."

"I can't believe Oscar Mayer shipped this over."

"It really means a lot that you guys are here."

While the customer interactions have been rewarding, I've decided this trip is more social experiment than marketing mission. What we're doing is commendable—bringing a taste of home to those families stationed overseas. And, yes, military families definitely buy more Oscar

Mayer products when we're parked outside the commissary. But I wonder if the expense of shipping a Wienermobile overseas (plus gas and the cost of feeding and housing two Hotdoggers) is offset by a small gain in Lunchables sales.

I say "social experiment" because I can't think of many other situations where two near-strangers have been tossed together and forced to spend six weeks traveling through foreign countries in a mobile hot dog. So far, Debbie and I have held up rather well. We're not best buddies, but we're far from enemies. I would say our partnership is somewhere in the "companion" phase. And that's about all you can ask for such strange circumstances. Having to rely on each other so much has definitely forced us to get along.

Like me, Debbie is of many moods. She just seems to cycle through hers faster. One minute it's "Dave, can you please hand me the whistle bag?"; the next it's "Dave! Hand me the whistle bag!"

The easiest way to get to know somebody is to tour Europe in a Wienermobile with them. Before we got on the road I had no idea that Debbie was such a neat freak. Pretty much every day I hear "Dave, can you pick up your tapes?" or "Dave, can you straighten out the luggage in the back?" I try not to get super aggravated because I know that Debbie just wants the Wienermobile to look presentable when we're on base. It must come from that military upbringing of hers.

Debbie, in turn, seems a bit puzzled by me at times. Like my insistence on flossing after meals. "You sure do that a lot," she says one day as I'm scrapping a fluoride string against my gums.

"Really?"

"Yeah. I've never seen anyone floss so much."

Debbie and I don't have many common interests. It's not like my travels with Ali, where we immediately bonded over a passion for fried food. Or my time with Sofia, where we spent hours swapping embarrassing stories.

A big sticking point for our new team has been music. Like

disagreements over food, disagreements over music can tear a team apart. Today, coming through the Wienermobile's tinny speakers I hear a booming chorus that proclaims, "Our God is an awesome God!" Oh no . . . Debbie likes Christian rock.

The notes hit my ears like daggers. I consider myself Christian, but I've never felt compelled to sing about God or Jesus or any sort of awesomeness. Normally, I'd just suffer in silence, fingernails digging into the relish-colored upholstery. This time, however, I decide to fight back the only way I know how—with passive aggressive sarcasm.

"Wow, this is great music," I say. Debbie raises an eyebrow, her focus still on the road. "Go God! Rock out!"

Eventually we reach our destination and get out of the vehicle. As I'm walking to the front door, Debbie blocks my path. "Listen," she says in a tone I haven't heard before. "I don't make fun of your music. Don't make fun of mine."

Debbie then pivots and walks purposefully away, leaving me to pick up my jaw.

CHAPTER 36

We've been in Germany for a few weeks and people still don't know what to make of the Wienermobile. The fun part of this trip has been driving through remote villages, the tiny hamlets you'd never see on a usual tourist's itinerary. The people in these places *really* have no idea what to make of the Wienermobile. The other day we passed a woman who was outside sweeping her stoop. She just stopped and stared, face void of all expression. Then there was the old man in a crisp gray suit and white hat standing on the corner. He saw us coming and suddenly lifted up his pants leg and stuck out his thumb like we was hitchhiking. That's probably the best reaction we've gotten so far.

While Germans are still getting used to us, it's worth noting that the Wienermobile is not just a U.S. phenomenon. Spain, Puerto Rico, and Japan each have one. Canada has two! So does Mexico. Coincidentally enough, one of the Mexican vehicles is HOTDOGG'N, the same Wienermobile we drove around California. Brad and Sofia dropped off HOTDOGG'N at the border when they were done their tour of Hispanic grocery stores in Texas. I often wonder how HOTDOGG'N is doing now. I hope the Mexican Hotdoggers are taking good care of her.

Our German hub, and the place we've spent the most time, is the picturesque city of Wurzburg. Located on the Main River, between Frankfurt and Nuremberg, Wurzburg almost shouldn't exist anymore. On March 16, 1945, more than two hundred British bombers used incendiary bombs to level the city in a matter of minutes. Five thousand people died in the ensuing firestorm, and most of the dwellings were destroyed.

It took more than twenty years, but the city was eventually rebuilt. Now, Wurzburg has about 130,000 residents who happily move about the reconstructed churches, cathedrals, and historic sites. If you didn't know better, you'd swear every building was a sparkling original rather than a faithful copy.

Debbie lived in Wurzburg while her dad was stationed in nearby Giebelstadt. We drive through her old neighborhood as she giddily reminisces: "That's my old swing set! That's the corner where we used to dance to Madonna! Oh! That's my old house! Let's stop! Let's stop!"

We pull the Wienermobile to the front of the house and I wait in the car while Debbie skips up the front steps. A woman opens the door and does a double take at the vehicle parked outside. While she and Debbie talk, the woman keeps looking over Debbie's shoulder to make sure she's really seeing a Wienermobile. After a few minutes, Debbie returns.

"What happened?" I asked.

"Well, I told her that I used to live here, but she wouldn't let me look inside. Said it was too messy."

"She was probably just scared of the giant hot dog parked outside her house."

We stop by Debbie's old elementary school, where I'm coerced into taking pictures of her next to everything that might have even a trace of sentimentality—the playground, the soccer field, the water fountain. The reception at the elementary school is much better than the one at

Debbie's old house. Kids (and quite a few teachers) press against their classroom windows to get a better look at the Wienermobile.

Debbie is even able to reconnect with her old music teacher, whom she describes as "one of the most influential teachers in my life." I can only imagine how she explained returning to Wurzburg fourteen years later in a Wienermobile.

I'm glad to be able to see some of Debbie's past. It makes me better appreciate her in the present. Once you get past the shiny Christian veneer, Debbie can be a lot of fun. We recently went out drinking in Bamburg, yet another in a series of historic towns with great beer. The specialty in Bamburg is smoked beer, which tastes a lot like ham. The aftertaste is initially overpowering, but you hardly notice it after four or five drinks. Debbie somehow drank me under the table. She got so drunk that she bummed a cigarette off an amused bar patron and then proceeded to light the wrong end.

Yes, we're getting paid to relive childhood memories and drink our way through Germany. I'm really going to be sad when this job ends.

CHAPTER 37

Italy has a long and storied sausage history. Many of our most popular sausages are named after the Italian cities where they originated: Bologna, Genoa, Milano, and Salami. Yet drive a Wienermobile through northern Italy and you'll swear that these people have never seen a sausage before. Stares, more frightened than friendly, are the norm. Some people don't even register our existence at all, choosing instead to stay focused on the windy mountain roads that cut through pristine northern valleys. Such driving may be safer, but it's no fun.

After three weeks in Germany, Debbie and I are heading to Aviano Air Base for the first of two northern Italian events. We're both a little nervous about going to a new country since we've only just figured out Germany. But that's life with the Wienermobile, never allowing you a chance to get comfortable.

Yesterday we took a stunning drive through the Alps on our way to Austria. Once again, my pessimistic mind anticipated breaking down on a steep pass and having to kill mountain goats for sustenance. But that didn't happen, and the Alps let us pass without incident. Now we'll see if Italy will be so kind.

"We should probably stop for gas," says Debbie.

"Sure, whatever," I respond. I'm already a bit moody since Debbie just made me pull over and take a picture of her in front of the WELCOME TO ITALY sign. What a waste of precious drive time. But as much as I'd like to blow past the gas station to spite my partner, I'd rather not stall on the side of this mountain highway.

We pull into our first Italian gas station and are immediately met by a uniformed attendant. The man could not be any more confused. We look down and see him shaking his head and then raising his arms and then shaking his head and then raising his arms. This goes on for a while.

"What do you think he wants?" asks Debbie.

"I'm not sure. Maybe he's just happy to see us."

"He doesn't look happy."

And then I remember something our German contact mentioned—most Italian gas stations are full service. The attendant is trying to figure out how to pump gas into a hot dog.

Debbie opens the gull wing door and the man walks over. "Cosa benzina? Cosa benzina?" Debbie just shrugs, so the attendant becomes even more animated. He points to the gas pump. "Cosa benzina?!"

"I think he wants to know what gas to put in," says Debbie.

"Geez, I don't know." I walk over and look at the pump. It's a dizzying array of colors and letters that I'm hopeless at deciphering. "Unleaded?" I say to the attendant. He again throws his hands up in frustration and begins to pace next to the Wienermobile. This is all very stressful.

Debbie and I study the pump for a while. We're going to have to figure this out on our own. "I say we go with the green button," I say. "Green means go."

"What about yellow?"

"I don't know what yellow is."

"But you know what green is?"

"No, but green seems safest. Plus, most of the other cars here are using green."

"Okay, let's go with green," agrees Debbie.

I get the attendant's attention and point to the green button. "We want this one . . . this one. Green!" The attendant nods his head affirmatively, unhooks the nozzle, and sullenly begins pumping the gas.

"I hope this is right," I say.

"Me, too," says Debbie.

After paying with our trusty American Express card, I get behind the wheel, turn the key, and brace for impact. The engine starts and, more importantly, doesn't blow up. I look at a relieved Debbie and smile. Always go green.

Fuel is not the only cultural barrier facing us in Italy. There's also dinner. After a long drive to Aviano, we're both looking forward to some authentic Italian food. But the restaurant's menu is in Italian, for some reason. I guess we erred too far on the authentic side. Debbie and I both order something with "pollo" in it, because we know that's chicken. Debbie, excited about drinking in another country, also orders a whole carafe of wine. For herself.

Since we've spent the entire day together, we don't say much at dinner. Really, what is there to say? So we sit in silence, both secretly wishing we were somewhere else. Or with someone else.

The problem with eating in Europe is that it takes forever. I understand wanting to enjoy the experience, but at some point you just want to stand up and scream, "Give me my food! I have a life to get back to!"

After an eternity, our meals finally arrive. "Is this it?" asks a perplexed Debbie. In front of her is a microscopic portion of chicken and carrots. We're talking a chicken strip and one baby carrot. I'd laugh, but my entrée is served in a thimble.

The waitress then brings the wine, which is in a container so large that it eclipses Debbie's plate. "Well, at least you can drink dinner," I say.

"Yeah, guess I'm gonna have to."

With little food and an abundance of wine, it doesn't take long before Debbie is slurring her words. "This is messed up," she says. "I don't want to be in Italy anymore. They don't eat here."

Meeting us the next morning is Eric, our Italian sales rep. Eric is a force of nature—a bundle of energy tenuously stored in a short, bald package. "The Wienie conquered the Alps!" he proclaims when we pull in.

The great thing about the S&K reps is that they don't fit the corporate model. Ed, our Frankfurt contact, bought us groceries, invited us over for dinner, and toasted us with premium schnapps. Chris in Wurzburg snuck us onto the base after hours so we could check e-mail and do laundry. These are fun, gregarious people who seem completely devoted to making sure we're well taken care of. It's nice to be so loved.

Eric looks more biker than businessman. He wears a thick leather jacket and pants with way too many pockets. His head is perfectly round and totally bald, a plump peach with no fuzz. Black glasses supply a thoughtful counterbalance to what otherwise could be a menacing first impression. But spend only a few seconds with Eric and you'll quickly realize that he's a teddy bear.

Eric has engineered a marketing masterstroke for our event in Aviano—see the Oscar Mayer Wienermobile and receive a free Lunchables. It's a plan that appeals to both frugal moms and hungry kids, meaning that we're swamped the entire day. Debbie and I spend most of the shift pressed back to back, rapidly tossing out whistles and making sure no overly caffeinated kids sneak into the Wienermobile.

Toward the end of the day, Eric approaches and asks a favor. A fellow S&K employee has a young daughter who attends a nearby Italian school. "Would you guys mind driving over there tomorrow so that the kids can have a look?"

"Hmmm, tomorrow?" stammers Debbie.

"Tomorrow, huh? Let's see. I'm not sure . . ." I say.

It's a tall order because tomorrow is our day off and I was looking forward to sitting in my hotel room and watching unintelligible TV. But since our S&K reps have been such generous hosts, we give in and agree to help out. I may be selfish, but I'm not a complete jerk.

For our troubles, Eric personally tours us around Venice. Having a local lead you around makes all the difference. Eric cuts us through narrow alleys and over creaky bridges, advises us to avoid the overpriced souvenir stores, and buys us lunch at a hidden restaurant well off the beaten path.

While we're eating, I ask Eric, "Why do meals last so long here?"

"Because people here like to digest their food," he answers matter-of-factly.

"Yeah, but why are the portions so small?" asks Debbie.

"What do you mean?"

"Well, we had dinner the other night and I ordered chicken and they just gave me a tiny piece."

"Is that all you ordered?"

"Yeah."

"There's your problem. In Italy, they eat in courses. You have to order your first course and then your second course and vegetables are a whole different course."

"Oh. Well that's good to know."

Venice is a maze, but one you're happy to get lost in. Before leaving, we spend some time feeding pigeons in St. Mark's Square. "It's touristy, but you have to do it," says Eric.

The next morning, Debbie and I arrive at the Italian school early and are told by Pam, the S&K mom, to wait in the parking lot while the nuns round up the children.

"Nuns?" I ask.

"Oh . . . yes," she says. "This is a Catholic school. It's run by an order of Italian nuns."

No one mentioned any nuns when we agreed to this field trip. I worry that a sausage this big is somehow sacrilege.

To kill time before our big unveiling, Debbie meticulously cleans

BIGBUN's messy windows (which are always messy since the wipers don't work) while I lazily polish the buns. My scrubbing is interrupted by a soft, delicate ding. I look over to see an elderly woman walking her bicycle toward us. The Wienermobile pulls her in like a tractor beam.

The woman is miniature and stooped by age; her bony arms are crisscrossed with thick blue veins that tremble slightly from supporting the oversized bike. A full head of gray hair suggests she's seen a lot in her life—but never anything like this. Her right hand, wrinkled and unsteady, reaches out to touch the Wienermobile's smooth surface.

"Que bella," she says in a soft voice. *How beautiful.*

She runs her hands along the fiberglass as her eyes dance across the polished exterior. At last she notices me and ambles closer.

"Hello," I say in a loud voice, as if that will somehow aid understanding.

She just smiles. Her eyes return to the Wienermobile, as if she's afraid this is an illusion that will soon disappear. The woman pats BIGBUN with affection. She looks up at me and starts speaking . . . rapidly and in Italian. By inflection, I'm guessing these are questions, but it's just a guess. I can pick out only a few scattered words, most of which I've gleaned from restaurant menus.

When she finally pauses for a breath, I jump into the conversation. "Parla inglese?" I ask.

She looks me in the eyes and sadly shakes her head "no." If only we had printed up informational cards in Italian. I gesture to the open door. "Would you like to see inside?" She nods her head "yes" and, after carefully propping up her *bicicletta*, walks inside. I follow behind and try explaining the situation to Debbie.

"You don't speak any Italian, do you?"

"No," she says. "Do you?"

"Uh, no. That's why I'm asking you."

Our visitor tilts her head in wonder, as if this were the Sistine

Chapel instead of a fiberglass hull. The woman, still searching for answers, turns to me with a thoughtful look in her eyes. "Español?"

Spanish. Of course!

I took three years of college Spanish. But when you go to college in white-bread Columbia, Missouri, there aren't many places to practice. And classes never covered any situation like this. Upon learning Sofia was bilingual, I assumed she'd teach me her native tongue. Of course, that never happened. The only useful phrase she shared was "Si compras tres productos de Oscar Mayer, les regalamos un juegete de beanbag." *If you buy three Oscar Mayer products, we'll give you a beanbag toy.*

"Que es esto?" she asks. *What is this?*

A good question, but one that is totally beyond my rudimentary language skills. I scramble to form something resembling a sentence. "Es un coche de salchicas." *It's a car of hot dogs.* Not very eloquent (and not totally accurate), but the woman lights up in recognition. And then she's off to the races.

I understand very little of what she rattles off next as it's very fast and very Spanish. I interject a polite "si" whenever there's a pause, but my comprehension is next to nothing. I imagine she's sharing both the joy and wonder of seeing this most American of automobiles. She's proud that our countries, enemies when she was a girl, can now trade smiles and culture so easily. Or maybe she's describing a trip to the dentist. I really don't know.

The woman eventually tires of talking and I help her outside. She takes a last look at BIGBUN and then carefully balances on her bicycle and starts off. Before disappearing around the corner, the elderly woman rings her bell three times.

"Did you see that?" I brag to Debbie. "I explained the Wienermobile to an Italian woman in Spanish."

"I'm very proud of you," says Debbie.

"There's really nothing I can't do."

"Yup, you're pretty amazing."

We don't get long to bask in this beautiful exchange of culture. Soon after our new friend peddles away, we're told that it's time to meet the children.

Driving the Wienermobile into a throng of kids is not one of my favorite things. Children are small and fast—making them easy to run over. Debbie and I play our usual game.

"Do you want to drive?"

"I don't care. Do you want to drive?"

"I don't care. Do *you* want to drive?"

Eventually, Debbie loses patience and agrees to get behind the wheel. I stand guard by the door, in case any of the children should pry open the lock and dart inside. It's happened.

Debbie does a smooth semicircle turn from the parking lot to a narrow, grassy patch behind the school. I brace myself for the piercing screams and carnal shouts. But there's just the steady hum of our engine.

"This it?" I ask.

"Oh yeah," answers Debbie. "This is it."

Still disbelieving, I twist the latch and let fly the hefty door. Cautiously, I peek my head outside. Standing on the playground grass are about thirty children. Each one wears a pastel smock in yellow, blue, or pink. Now, here's the scary part. The children don't move, don't blink, and don't make a sound. It's like zombie recess.

Pam, the mother we're here to help, walks over and introduces me to the head nun, a tall, imposing figure dressed all in black. With no idea how to properly introduce a nun to a Wienermobile, I just politely bow a few times.

The nun says a few soft words in Italian. What's with everyone in this country speaking a foreign language? Pam steps in and translates. "They would like to show the children inside."

"Um ... well ... we don't usually—"

The head nun takes this as an invitation. Before I can object, she and her subordinate sisters divide the students into small groups and shepherd them toward the Wienermobile. I'm relieved to see the statue children move, but I'm also worried about having them all inside, climbing over our delicate fineries.

Debbie, meanwhile, is having problems of her own. An incoming wave of besmocked boys and girls traps her near the steering wheel. Unable to exit, she offers me a "what's going on?" look through the window. I respond with an "I don't know" shrug. In no time, the nuns have packed fifteen children into the Wienermobile. Now that's Italian efficiency.

And then an amazing thing happens: nothing. The children, some huddled together on relish seats, others standing on the ketchup walkway, remain totally still. The tweeting birds are louder than these kids.

The first group gets a strict minute to soak up the ambiance. Then a nun's sharp handclap signals that it's time to go. The children turn toward the door and, one by one, march down the steps in rigid precision. I wait outside and hand them each a Wiener Whistle, which no one dares to blow.

All the children get a turn sitting inside BIGBUN. It's hard to tell if they enjoy the experience since no one smiles and no one talks.

"Do you think we should show them how to use the whistles?" asks Debbie.

"If you want. This doesn't really seem like a whistling group."

Debbie bravely wades into the sea of students, crouches down to their level, and patiently demonstrates how to whistle a whistle.

Toot! Toot!

The children, a bit surprised by the sudden noise, all look to the nuns for guidance. After a tense moment of consideration, the head nun stifles a smile and nods her approval. The kids let loose. Twenty minutes of pent-up exuberance is quickly channeled through tiny whistles.

Toot! Toot! Toot! Toot!

This is Gabriel's trumpet, Oscar Mayer style.

A few days later, Eric gives us a parting gift from the Aviano base—a collection of drawings and letters from Miss Bishop's second grade class. While we were at the base, Miss Bishop brought her students by for a visit. These children were energetic, loud, and very inquisitive. In other words, completely different from the Catholic kids. But we still enjoyed showing them around the Wienermobile.

We're often asked why the Wienermobile doesn't stop at more schools. I think it's because Oscar Mayer doesn't want to appear like some corporate ogre that's trying to brainwash kids. But after reading the notes from Miss Bishop's class, I wish that we did make more school stops. No one appreciates the Wienermobile more than a second grader.

What Miss Bishop's class lacks in basic knowledge of spelling and grammar, they more than make up for in heartfelt gratitude. A few of the more awesome comments (spelling mistakes included):

Thank you Oscarmobile for the whistle and for looking at the Oscarobile. We will came agin some day the outside and the inside we all liked.

I liked it a lot it was cool. I'de like to look at it again but I can't.

We like Big Bun. He is very cute.

Thank you for letting us see the Wienermobile. That was very generous and kind of you.

It looks so cool I wish I can have it but I do not no think my mom or dad would not like it.

Thank you for letting us in your Wienermobile. It was so yummy.

I will always remember the whner mobel.

CHAPTER 38

I t didn't take long before the '95 Wienermobiles started showing their age. In 1999, Oscar Mayer had extra money in the
budget and the head of marketing asked Russ if they could
get two Wienermobiles built "real quick." "Nothing with the
Wienermobile is 'real quick,'" replied Russ.

But with only a few months before the money disappeared from
the budget, Russ was forced to move fast. He contracted with Craftsmen
Industries, a St. Louis company that has built custom vehicles for everyone from Pringles to Chiclets.

The same company that did the fiberglass work for the '88 Wienermobiles was brought in to work on the '00s. The door design was
changed, scrapping the troublesome hydraulic lift, and a 5700 Vortec
engine was dropped in under the hood. Otherwise, the '00 models
were almost exact replicas of the 1995s—same interior, same seating,
same chassis.

The '00 Wienermobiles made their debut in Madison Square
Garden, along with a new version of Talent Search in which people had to
make up their own jingles. The Boys Choir of Harlem and R&B performer
Monica helped welcome the new dogs.

Just like us mammals, the Wienermobile continues to evolve.

In 2004, Oscar Mayer debuted an updated model made by Prototype Source in Santa Barbara, California. It's built on a GMC W-series chassis, same as the '00 model. But the '04s have more power, with GM's 5.7-liter V8 Vortec engine. They also sport slick Pontiac Firebird headlights.

The '04s look similar to the '00s on the outside but have a completely redesigned interior. The main cabin is now one level, meaning you don't have to trip onto the drivers' platform anymore. The six chairs are no longer relish green; instead they're bold, unapologetic ketchup red and mustard yellow. The side rhomboids are cleverly transparent, adding two new windows for those passengers in the way back. The ceiling is covered with a cool, if thematically awkward, blue-sky mural. Gone is the entertainment system. In its place is an interactive display called Oscartown. I'm not sure what Oscartown is for, but I bet the Hotdoggers miss having a big TV in the back.

The '04s also have one of the most annoying features ever included on a Wienermobile: a jingle horn. As if the world needs that.

In 2008, the company needed something special to celebrate 125 years of business. Thus was born the mini Wienermobile. Built by adding a fiberglass hot dog mold on top of a Mini Cooper S frame, the "cocktail" Wienermobile is only fifteen feet long and gets much better gas mileage than its larger brethren. With chrome hubcaps, two doors, and a sleek style, this Wienermobile proves that size really doesn't matter.

CHAPTER 39

All it does is rain. My throat hurts. I think I've got an ear infection. The pillows are lumpy. Breakfast is a plate of cold meats. Debbie is bugging me. I miss America.

The mark of a true Hotdogger is the ability to complain even when you're on an all-expenses paid trip to Europe. Here we are, weeks into the work adventure of a lifetime, and I'm consumed with thoughts of going home. I've had fun, but six weeks is a long time to be a stranger in a strange land.

The trip so far has been a mix of good and bad. Good has been the extensive sightseeing. We've toured a Salzburg salt mine, taken a bus trip through the Alps, biked around Munich, hoisted a stein at the historic Munich Hofbräuhaus, walked the rebuilt streets of Berlin, visited the picturesque Castle Neuschwanstein (the model for Cinderella's castle at Disneyland), sipped wine in Wurzburg, played with the pigeons in Venice, and sang "Like a Virgin" at a karaoke pub in Trier.

On the flip side, there has been a series of random misfortunes, which seem to affect only me. First there's been the constant sore throat. Then I backed the Wienermobile into a light pole, leaving a long, green streak down the middle of the right side bun. Then there was our return drive from Italy to Germany. Going over the Alps we approached a narrow tollbooth.

"Are you sure you can fit?" asked Debbie.

"Sure! No sweat." I said with much bravado.

As we got closer to the booth, however, I began to doubt my optimistic assessment. The tollbooth operator doubted it, too. She ran out of the booth, stood in the middle of the lane, and frantically waved her arms back and forth, begging me to stop. But since we fit through on the initial leg, I waved her off. The woman shook her head, muttered some Italian obscenities, and returned to her booth.

Turns out, she was right. As I inched the Wienermobile into the toll lane, trying to stay as centered as possible, I noticed tiny sparks coming from where the bun scraped against the metal side rails.

"Oops," I said.

"Uh, Dave—"

But it was too late. I had to push the Wienermobile through, further squeezing the sausage. When I at last inched to the tollbooth, the collector was not happy. She frowned deeply as I sheepishly handed her some money. When we got out the other side, I pulled over and saw that the buns really had been scratched badly. I hoped Russ wouldn't notice.

My most recent misadventure involved some rotten meat. No, it wasn't a bad hot dog. Instead, I made an ill-advised attempt to sample local cuisine and ordered venison goulash for dinner. The only positive thing about my night of cramped, vomiting horror was the heated floor in my hotel bathroom. Trust me—I spent a lot of time on that floor.

The next morning I woke up and couldn't feel my legs. Debbie had to help me onto the Wienermobile and then prop me up in the backseat. I didn't move the entire day. People would peek their heads in and see an incapacitated stranger weakly waving at them. Very few smiles were shared that day.

It does seem trivial to complain about such petty things, but I'm worn out and ready to be done, not only with Europe, but with the

Wienermobile, too. Now I understand why this job lasts for only one year—any longer and you'd go mad. Right now, an endless stretch of unemployment seems preferable to another day spent spouting hot dog puns.

But ask me again after a few weeks living back home with my parents.

"You figure out what you're going to do next?" I ask Debbie as she's driving us through the picturesque German countryside.

"No, not really. You?"

"I have no idea. Are you nervous?" I ask.

"Nope. When you face as many challenges as we have on the road and you make so many decisions on your own, you just go with it."

"Well said."

"Are you nervous?"

I take a moment to consider this. I have every reason to be nervous: no job, no prospects, and still no future path. Yet as we pass another confused German motorist, I feel strangely at peace. "No," I answer. "I'm not really nervous."

Debbie offers me one of her bright, assuring smiles. "Hey, if we can drive a Wienermobile through Europe, we can do anything."

In the end, every dog has its last day.

Schinnen Army Base in the Netherlands is the site of our final event. This last event is no different than every other event we've done over the last year. We pass out whistles, answer questions with bad puns, and try to avoid looking bored. Debbie, ever worried about cleanliness, gives the windows a final scrub. I wander around taking black and white pictures, hoping to accurately capture our melancholy mood.

The day concludes with no fanfare, probably because we're the only ones who know this is the end. Packing up takes a bit longer, either because we're overly exhausted or because we're trying to savor the moment. Cargo safely stored, I shoo away the remaining stragglers and pull down the heavy door. I jump in the driver's seat and fish through khaki shorts for my lucky keychain.

"Ready to go?" asks Debbie.

I'm not sure I am ready, but I suppose we can't stay in Schinnen forever. "Ready to go."

The events may be over, but there's plenty of driving to do. We still have to get BIGBUN back to Frankfurt, where it will be loaded onto a boat for the long trip home.

Debbie gets uncharacteristically excited as we approach the German border. "We've got to pull over and take a picture!" she shrieks.

"Of what?"

"Of the Germany sign!"

"Really? Do we have to?" I moan.

"Yes, we do. Pull over."

Because the welcome sign is coming up fast, I have to swerve across three lanes of traffic to reach the shoulder in time. Somehow I don't roll the dog, and we pull up next to the giant blue road sign reading BONDS-REPUBLIEK DUITSLAND.

"Alright, let's make this quick," I tell Debbie as we skid to a stop. She responds with a sarcastic smirk and hurries out the door with her camera. I grab mine and follow a few steps behind.

Outside, Debbie is already framing her shot. "Can you shut the door?" she asks, "It's blocking the sign."

I slam the door shut and then wade through a patch of weeds to get a few pictures of the Wienermobile returning to Germany. Debbie's right—it is a cool shot. BIGBUN's bright colors contrast nicely with the metallic sign. This could be a postcard.

Satisfied with our artistic efforts, we return to the Wienermobile, eager to finish our farewell voyage. There's just one problem: Debbie can't get the door open.

After several attempts, she gives up and turns to me, sweat beading on her forehead. "Did you lock the door?"

"I don't think so. Here, let me try."

Confident that we just need more muscle, I nudge Debbie aside and take my turn at the latch. Once again, Debbie's right. This door is definitely locked.

And then there's another problem. In my haste to save time, I left the Wienermobile running. Oh, and the external speakers are on, blaring Fleetwood Mac's *Rumors* album across the autobahn.

"How do we get in?" asks Debbie.

"I have no idea."

There are only two options: climbing through a window or dropping through the bunroof. The windows, however, slide open only wide enough to accommodate a newborn infant.

"Maybe we left the bunroof open," I say hopefully. But after scaling BIGBUN, I discover that no, we did not leave the bunroof open.

Not only are we locked out with the engine running, but our belongings are trapped inside. We have no cell phone and no way to summon help. In America, someone might pull over to help, but on the autobahn, everyone is slightly scared of this mobile sausage.

Debbie has been studying the situation. "I think if we unscrew this bar we can open the window more and maybe I can slide in."

Looking at the window, she might be onto something. There's a small metallic rod that stops the window from sliding open all the way. Remove it and we could be in business. Too bad neither of us has a screwdriver.

It's then that I notice a Shell station on the horizon. I offer to play hero. "I'll run up there and see if I can borrow a screwdriver. Be right back..."

With "Don't Stop (Thinking about Tomorrow)" appropriately playing in the background, I begin my lonely jog. A few minutes later, I stagger through the front door of the service station. The attendant snaps to attention, probably worried that I'm here to rob the place.

"English?" I stammer between deep breaths.

"Yes?" he replies, still unsure who or what I am.

I try explaining the situation as best I can without going into the whole "we're locked out of our Wienermobile" thing. "My friend and I are having some car trouble up the road and so I was wondering if I could borrow a screwdriver."

"Ein screwdriver?"

"Well, we're trying to open a door but there's a little rod that we need to unscrew first."

"Ein rod?"

"Yes, ein rod," I reply while trying to pantomime the word.

"Why do you need open door?" he asks. This guy's a real Sherlock Holmes.

"Because we stopped to take pictures and got locked out of our car."

"Why stop to take pictures?"

"I don't know. It seemed like a good idea at the time."

"Okay," he says, after some soul searching. "But I need something until you return." The man looks me over. "Your watch."

"My watch?" A Seiko watch that my parents gave me for graduation in return for a rusty screwdriver? That hardly seems fair.

"Your watch," he repeats. "I give it back when you return screwdriver."

With no room to negotiate, I slowly slide over the watch.

I sprint back to the Wienermobile, holding the screwdriver like an Olympic torch. The return jog is slow and labored, showing just how much this sedentary lifestyle has damaged my cardiovascular health. But seeing the Wienermobile grow larger on the horizon inspires me to continue.

I make it back and breathlessly hand off the screwdriver to Debbie before collapsing against the bun. Debbie works the screws for a moment before turning to me. "Dave, this is the wrong size."

"I'm sorry (pant, pant) . . . I didn't (pant, pant) . . ."

Debbie takes pity on me. "I'll go back."

"Thanks," I whimper.

My normal breathing returns about the same time Debbie does. She hands me the new screwdriver, which is just as rusty as the first one. Like a nervous surgeon, I delicately begin the operation. The rod comes off easily and I slide the window until it's fully dilated. The opening is a bit bigger, but still pretty narrow. I look over to Debbie, who is already nervously pacing. She knows what's next.

"You ready?" I ask.

"You think I can fit?"

"I know I can't."

Debbie nods in grim acceptance of her fate. I crouch down to offer my body as a human stepladder. Debbie pushes off my back and quickly gets her head and arms through the opening. The easy part is over.

I stand up to see Debbie half in and half out of the Wienermobile. Her legs kick the air wildly, trying desperately to create some kind of forward momentum. It's not happening. Debbie is stuck. This is a brilliant, if slightly scary, scene—my partner wedged into the tiny window opening.

"Dave, help!" she yells, her voice nearly lost in the still-blaring Fleetwood Mac soundscape. She alternates between wild laughter and pained yelps.

"What do you want me to do?"

"Push!"

There's no going back so I grab her legs and shove. Khaki fabric rustles against the metal window frame. It's not a happy sound.

"Keep pushing!"

I wrap my arms around her ankles and make one last desperate shove. Pop! Debbie surges forward and tumbles hard to the Wienermobile floor. I peek my head through the window and see Debbie, sprawled on the ketchup and mustard walkway, laughing like a little child while rubbing her bruised hips.

Debbie opens the door and we spend a good five minutes laughing about our stupidity. Finally composed, we drive to the Shell station so I can recover my watch. The ever-attentive attendant notices our unusual ride outside. "Is that your auto?" he asks in wonderment.

"Yes," I say on my way out. That's the only explanation he's going to get.

Our picture detour cost us an hour of time and many gallons of gas. The best part? After getting back on the autobahn, we soon come upon a sign that reads WELCOME TO GERMANY.

"That's strange," I say. "I wonder why they've got two signs."

It's only after the pictures are developed that we notice the sign we went through hell to photograph actually reads REPUBLIC OF GERMANY—1 KM.

We photographed the wrong sign.

CHAPTER 40

It's a day I knew was coming, yet never believed would arrive—the day we drop off the Wienermobile.

There's a shocking amount of emotion as I drive us to the Frankfurt warehouse that will ship BIGBUN home. This is the last time I'll ever get behind the wheel of a Wienermobile, the last time I'll ever be recognized by the car I drive.

Debbie and I, both lost in personal reflection, don't say much on the way. It's almost like we're driving to a funeral. In a way, it is the death of a very unique way of life. No more bouncing from town to town, having our meals paid for and people cleaning up after us.

This is the end of a responsible type of irresponsibility. With no one left to pay for my travels, I'm being forced to settle down and find a real job. What that job will be, I still have no idea. The plan was to use this year to discover a direction in life. Between the county fairs and the breakdowns and the side trips and the whistles and the Walmarts, that plan didn't pan out.

But while I didn't find a path, I did find the confidence to find a path. I didn't even try for this job, and yet I still beat out thousands of applicants. I survived a night in a New Orleans jail. I communicated with carnies. I learned how to parallel park a twenty-seven-foot-long hot dog. I conquered the Alps. With those skills, there's not much I can't do.

The Wienermobile taught me not to stress so much. Sorry to overuse travel metaphors, but life is like a long road trip. There are breakdowns and there are beautiful distractions, but there's no real road map. You just make a right here, a left there, and see what happens.

And when the road ends, you move back home with your parents.

We pull into the barren warehouse parking lot and are met by a gruff, round man in pale overalls. The man lazily waves us toward a corner of the lot, barely looking up from his clipboard and morning cigarette. I drive us into the spot and put the Wienermobile in park. With a heavy heart, I turn off the engine.

There's a Wienermobile tradition that I've been looking forward to the entire year—signing the inside of the dog. On the walls of the back storage area, safely beyond public view, are autographed reminders from Hotdoggers past. It's the Oscar Mayer equivalent of cave drawings. Now it's our turn to add to this illustrated history.

Debbie hands me the black Sharpie pen and I awkwardly angle my body so that I can etch the ceiling. How Michelangelo did it, I'll never know.

My message to future generations:

5/29/00

BIGGIE—

"With your chrome heart shining in the sun, long may you run."

—Neil Young. Dave Ihlenfeld XII

Epilogue

While dropping off the Wienermobile was emotional, it was a sunny walk in the park compared with our last days in Madison. The old gang laughed, cried, and, of course, hugged. In between, we gamely tried to get as drunk as possible. It's hard to believe thirteen people, bound only by a common hot dog–shaped vehicle, could grow so close.

Saying good-bye to my girls, Ali and Sofia, was like losing two sisters in one day. We'll see each other again, but I will greatly miss passing the time with conversations about everything from sex to sandwiches.

I came into the Wienermobile a naïve innocent when it came to women. After several months with Ali and Sofia, I finally have a window into the feminine mystique. That's not to say I understand women. But at least I now have a vague idea about how menstuation works.

Saying goodbye to Russ, my road father, was also tough. I went to accept my "graduation" gift, a pewter statue of the Wienermobile, and actually got a bit choked up shaking the boss's hand.

"Thanks for everything, Russ. I really appreciate it," I said.

"Thank you, David," he responded. A man of few words, but the moment felt genuine.

Post-Wienermobile depression, a condition common among former Hotdoggers, hit early. My parents picked me up at the airport in our tan Toyota Corolla. We drove down a busy Chicago highway and no one waved to us, no one smiled, no one tried to follow us home.

For the first time in a year, I was a man without a hot dog.

The Wienermobile program rolls on, although it has hit a few bumps along the way.

In 2001, an '88 Wienermobile was traveling on I-15 north toward Victorville, California. While going up a steep incline, the Wienermobile started shaking and smoking. It then caught fire. The Hotdoggers escaped, but the Wienermobile burned to the ground. The Hotdoggers lost almost all their personal belongings.

Russ arrived a few days later to survey the wreckage. Oscar Mayer even hired a forensic engineer to study the charred remains (although only the frame and some melted fiberglass survived). The engineer concluded that transmission fluid had gotten on the engine manifold and stared the fire. As a result, the hoses and lines were replaced on all the (literally) hot dogs.

In 2004, Russ decided to leave Oscar Mayer to pursue other passions. It was a rather quiet, unexpected exit for the man who, more than anyone, built the Wienermobile Department into what it is now.

Russ had been involved with the Wienermobile since its relaunch in 1988 and was responsible for greatly growing the program. Russ modernized the fleet. He immediately realized that the '88s desperately needed to be replaced by more reliable Wienermobiles. The '95 Wienermobiles that Russ commissioned were a radical departure from previous models and are still used as the basis for today's Wienermobiles.

Under Russ, the Wienermobile program was a tight family. There was a ten-year reunion, and current Hotdoggers were required to look up alumni in whatever town they were visiting. With Russ gone, that sadly doesn't happen anymore.

Whatever became of Team California? Surprisingly, most of us are in California. Sofia, Brad, and I all live in Los Angeles. Sofia and Brad stopped dating shortly after he left the road. After so much time together, I think it was distance that did them in.

It wasn't until recently that I learned the specifics about how Brad and Sofia found love on the road. Over a few drinks, Brad finally spilled the sausage. "That first hotel in Stockton, I had chilled out in her room and we were just being flirty and I think I kissed her like right after that."

"So I never had a chance."

Brad just smiled. "I think it was probably that I was a little older than you. I had been on the road; I wasn't messing around. Plus I knew Spanish. There just wasn't a contest."

Brad is a stand-up comic who leads college students on tours of South America in his spare time. With a freshly shaved head he looks a bit like Bruce Willis. Since Brad lives clear across town, our paths don't cross often. No one in Los Angeles is willing to sit in maddening traffic just for some social contact. But I consider him a friend, rather than just a former coworker.

We all thought Brad and Sofia would get back together, but there doesn't seem to be much chance of that happening. Once you've known love on the road, a regular relationship must seem kind of boring.

Sofia's an actress who's constantly in motion. She's had about four hundred jobs (give or take) while living in Los Angeles, everything from running a chewing gum promotion to selling advertising in local papers. Somehow she manages to make it back to Argentina a few times a year, all while maintaining a rigorous workout schedule. Sofia and I hang out quite a bit. She's even agreed to marry me if we're both forty and still single. Which is a definite possibility.

Ali hit the opposite coast and settled in New York. She thought about acting and Broadway, but eventually settled on singing. She's already put out an album and is an in-demand performer. Her style veers from country to folk to rock, but even a music snob like myself has to admit that the girl has talent.

I wonder if Russ knew that he was putting together a Wienermobile full of entertainers. I bet he did.

Despite my paranoid apprehensions, Hot Dog Dave has found life after the Wienermobile. And just like my Wienermobile days, the journey has been long, overheated, and nothing resembling a straight line.

After getting off the road, I lived at home for a few months and had no luck finding a job. Then a friend in Los Angeles told me about a job coordinating the *Jeopardy* Clue Crew, a mobile tour that would round up contestants for the game show. The position sounded perfect—it played off my newfound experience with mobile marketing and would get me back to LA. I faxed my resume to the producers and they were unbelievably excited to talk with someone who had driven the Wienermobile.

This is it, I thought. *My ticket to fame and fortune.*

The producers wanted to interview me, but weren't willing to pay for my plane ticket to Los Angeles. I was faced with the difficult dilemma of either not pursuing the job or spending $700 on a last-minute airfare. After a making lengthy pro and con list, I bought the ticket.

My interview went very well. I regaled the producers with tales from the road and, for the first time, began to see what a valuable commodity this Wienermobile job was. They ended the interview by taking me to meet the executive producer of both *Wheel of Fortune* and *Jeopardy*.

"This is Dave. He drove the Oscar Mayer Wienermobile!"

After further dazzling the executive producer, I left feeling triumphant.

"Just swing by HR and your way out and fill out an application," said my host. "It was *so good* meeting you."

I practically skipped to HR, confident that this job was mine. And then I saw the application. It was right there on page 2: "Have you ever been convicted of a felony or misdemeanor?"

Beads of sweat pooled on my forehead as I flashed back to my night in a New Orleans jail. I felt nauseous and ugly. How was I supposed to answer this question? If I lied, would they find out? If I told the truth, would I still get offered the job? I had tried to put that ugly incident out of my mind and had never thought how it might affect my future. And yet here it was, affecting my future.

I decided to answer truthfully: *I was mistakenly arrested for public intoxication in New Orleans. Rather than staying and fighting the charges, I plead "no contest" and paid a small fine.*

Okay, not 100 percent honesty, but I hoped the creative wording would buy me some mercy. It didn't. I never heard another word from the *Jeopardy* people.

After that scare, I took the first job I got offered—a production assistant spot at Britannica.com in Chicago. They had a less probing application, but that job didn't last long before the Internet bubble burst and the company folded. I'll never forget my exit interview when the HR rep asked, "Is there anything else you need? Well, besides a job."

After three months of anxious unemployment, I got another Internet job, this time editing content for AOL Digital City. Cutting and pasting text all day was not fun, but at least it was mindless.

I had a revelation as my yearlong contract with AOL was coming to an end. I could continue bouncing between boring nine-to-five jobs or I could get serious and follow my passion for entertainment. So I bought the family minivan from my parents, hitched up a tiny trailer, and drove with my father to Los Angeles. The long, lethargic trip was eerily reminiscent of my Wienermobile days, although my dad and I had no arguments over placemats or Christian rock. And the Windstar didn't overheat once.

In hindsight, moving to LA without a job or a plan was a bit silly. But it was nothing compared with trying to fit a Wienermobile through an Italian tollbooth.

Most of my time in LA has been spent as a television assistant—getting coffee, picking up lunch, and avoiding eye contact. You know, all the things you go to college for. But I have had some success. I co-wrote episodes of *Malcolm in the Middle* and *Family Guy* and even managed to keep a girlfriend (for more than three weeks). Recently, I landed my first full-time job as a television writer. It only took eight years, but now I get to berate the assistants when my coffee's cold. It's a good feeling.

Epilogue

The other members of Hotdoggers XII have gone on to do great and varied things. Jamila got her doctorate in neuroscience; Ben got his in environmental health. Debbie recruits for Ohio State, while Luke works in alumni relations for Georgetown. Candace started her own pastry business, then went back into PR, and was named one of the most eligible bachelorettes in Fort Wayne, Indiana. Shawna worked as Hotdogger advisor after we got off the road and then returned to Washington, DC, for a job in PR. Leah rebounded from her early termination and stumbled into a lucrative career in video games. Derrick continues to help people, this time at the American Red Cross. Melissa somehow became a professional poker player. Jane . . . well, no one's quite sure what became of Jane.

Perhaps the most poetic update comes from Hotdogger Kristy, a holdover from year XI. She married Chad, a Penske mechanic she met because her Wienermobile blew a head gasket. They've been together more than eleven years and recently got married. Sadly, scheduling didn't allow for a Wienermobile at the wedding.

Regardless of where people ended up, everyone credits the Wienermobile with helping them get there.

"I think it set me up for success in every job that I've done since," says Melissa.

"It gives you a level of responsibility that you don't even realize you have until it's over," says Shawna.

"It feels like you're part of history. You learn to rely on yourself and your partners, and I think it's a good life lesson," says Candace.

"I felt confident enough and empowered enough to do what I wanted to do. When you face that many challenges and you have to make so many decisions on your own, you just go with it," says Debbie. "There's so much of this job that has made me who I am. I always tell people I would do it all over again if someone asked me to."

The lessons of the Wienermobile really become apparent only in hindsight. I didn't appreciate the amount of responsibility I was taking on, which is probably why I accepted the job in the first place. Working in a team, dealing with customers, replacing coolant—these were all foreign concepts when I started. It's a testament to Russ and his department for recognizing character qualities in us that we weren't even aware of yet.

Russ once told me about companies that would call him for references and ask about attendance. "It was always one of those things where I wanted to laugh. *Um, I saw them a few times a year. We hired them, we told them where they were supposed to go, and we just assumed that they would show up.*"

It was special to be a part of something so special. Even now, I'm amazed at the power of a mobile hot dog. I think communications executive David Armano put it best: "Everything about the Wienermobile is designed to be memorable . . . It's an object that connects people, gets them talking and, more important, gets them sharing stories."

One year with the Wienermobile granted me confidence, perspective, and a measure of inner peace. But, more importantly, it showed that I don't have to settle. Being a Hotdogger pointed to a life beyond soulless jobs and windowless cubes. That's one hell of a severance package.

Be happy, be creative, be free—and never forget your Hotdogger Oath.

Appendix:

THE WORLD, AS SEEN FROM A HOT DOG

Friendliest City: Blue Ash, Ohio
Hotdogger Melissa and I never meant to fall in love with Blue Ash. It was supposed to be just another anonymous city, a convenient place to stop on our way through Ohio. But it turned out to be oh so much more. Everywhere we went, the kind Blue Ashians greeted us with open arms. The hostess at the local Rock Bottom brewpub saw us drive up in the Wienermobile and bumped us to the front of a long Friday-night wait list. The next day, the manager at the local Residence Inn personally dropped us off at a nearby lake so we could use the paddleboats. Two hours later, she came back and picked us up!

Most Obnoxious Event:
Dade County Kids' Expo 2000—Madison, Wisconsin
Imagine cramming a small expo center with hundreds of parents and small children. Imagine a crowd so thick that it's hard to walk. Now imagine plopping an open Wienermobile in the middle of such chaos. It wasn't pretty. The kids treated the Wienermobile like a jungle gym—climbing over seats, crawling down the aisle, and touching *everything*. I had to physically restrain one girl after she wouldn't stop honking the horn. As one exhibitor put it, "That horn is getting to be a royal pain."

Biggest Letdown: Tie: Daytona 500/Mardi Gras
The Daytona 500 is just loud cars traveling very fast around an oval track. Mardi Gras is just loud frat guys traveling very slowly down Bourbon Street. Alcohol helps make both events only slightly tolerable.

Appendix

Best Jazz: Ace Hill at Sly McFly's—Monterey, California

Sly McFly's is the most unusual of jazz clubs. It's located on the famous Cannery Row, overlooking Monterey Bay. The theme is a strange mix of stained glass and antique automobile racing. Everything about the place seems carefully designed to snare the unsuspecting tourist. Which is how we ended up there. After a long day at the aquarium, we wandered in expecting an evening of Miller Lite and lukewarm chicken fingers, but came away having experienced something magical—Ace Hill. Ace was a legendary local pianist who crafted boogie melodies both effortless and inescapable. Backed by a tight band, Ace entranced the entire bar. Sly's is still around but, sadly, Ace passed away in 2005.

Strangest Night Out: The Hut—Jacksonville, North Carolina

The Hut is a Polynesian-themed nightclub located in one of the most un-Polynesian places on earth. When Sofia and I asked the stoned front desk attendant at our motel for a good place to get a drink, his response was immediate and emphatic: "Um, I guess you could try the Hut." On the way over, our cab driver regaled us with tales of his sexual exploits. "I get laid every two weeks! And I'll be damned if I'm paying for it." The Hut itself was a jungle of tiki, bamboo, and red lighting. The highlight was sipping a banana daiquiri and watching a large lesbian and her equally bulky girlfriend both hit on Sofia. After a few drinks, I whirled around the dance floor and had a towering African American woman yell: "Slow down! You're making me dizzy!"

Best Place to Celebrate Halloween:
Alice Cooperstown—Phoenix, Arizona

Alice Cooper may not have invented Halloween, but he's certainly perfected it. And every year his namesake club throws a huge bash to celebrate the holiday. Ali and I just happened to be in Phoenix on October 31 and so there was no question of where to go. We didn't have costumes, but we did have some connections. While waiting in line, someone handed us VIP passes and we were whisked away to a private balcony overlooking the costumed masses. And what costumes they were—a group of friends dressed like the castaways from *Gilligan's Island*, a high-heeled woman covered head to toe in silver. A local band, Roger Clyne and the Peacemakers, provided the soundtrack to our gawking. But the true highlight came when Alice Cooper himself stepped onstage to sing "I'm 18" and "No More Mr. Nice Guy." Seeing Alice among this backdrop of costumed chaos made his black leather outfit look relatively tasteful.

Best Castle: Heidelberg Castle, Germany

When castle cruising in Germany, most people head to King Ludwig's towering Neuschwanstein, the inspiration for Sleeping Beauty's Castle at Disneyland. But for all its outer beauty, Neuschwanstein is unfinished and fairly empty inside. Plus, you also have to brave long lines and walk up an actual hill to even get to the place.

No, the real gem of the German castles can be found in Heidelberg. This also requires a walk uphill, but at least you won't feel like a schmuck when you get there. Unlike stark Neuschwanstein, Heidelberg Castle is alive and bustling, with plenty to see and explore. The castle overlooks the beautiful Neckar River. Try timing your visit to watch as the setting sun casts colorful shadows across the river valley.

Bibliography

Alesia, Tom. "Newest Member of Wienermobile Fleet Is Bite-Sized." *Wisconsin State Journal*, August 6, 2008.

Anonymous. "Industrial Strength Design: How Brooks Stevens Shaped Your World." Milwaukee Art Museum. http://www.mam.org/exhibitions/_sites/brooks/photos.asp.

———. "The Jeep Wienermobile." Wx4. http://wx4.org/to/wagons/weirdwillys/wienermobilex/wienermobile_history.html

———. "Brooks Stevens." Wisconsin History. http://www.wisconsinhistory.org.

———. "Meat Packer Oscar F. Mayer Is Dead at 95." *Chicago Daily Tribune*, March 12, 1955, B7.

———. "Oscar Mayer." January 1, 2001. http://www.findagrave.com/cgi-bin/fg.cgi?page=gr&GRid=712.

———. "Oscar Mayer Foods Corp." *International Directory of Company Histories*. Thomson Gale. 1996. Encyclopedia.com. http://www.encyclopedia.com/doc/1G2-2841600128.html.

———. "Refinancing of Oscar Mayer House Is Told." *Chicago Daily Tribune*, September 7, 1919, A13.

———. "The Wiener Men." *Retail Merchandiser*, August 2005, 16.

———. "Wurst for Wares." *Time*, April 12, 1968, 117.

———. "Wienermobile: The Inside Story," *Chicago Tonight*. First broadcast May 4, 2006 by WTTW Television, Chicago.

Armano, David. "What Brands Can Learn from a Wiener." *Advertisting Age* website, December 8, 2008. http://adage.com/digitalnext/post?article_id=133102.

Bibliography

Deleon, Clark. "It's Not Your Father's Wienermobile: Relish a Link with the Past." *Seattle Times*, February 24, 1995. http://community.seattletimes.nwsource.com/archive/?date=199502 24&slug=2106822.

Hinckley, Jim, and Ben G. Robinson. *The Big Book of Car Culture*. St. Max, MN: Motorbooks, 2005.

Kanfer, Stefan. "The Decline and Fill of the American Hot Dog." *Time*, October 2, 1972.

Kannapell, Andrea. "Hot Diggity! Dog Diggity!—Hotdoggers: Taking the Wiener to the World." *New York Times*, May 24, 1998, NY/Region section.

Kraig, Bruce. *Hot Dog: A Global History*. London: Reaktion, 2009.

Leroux, Charles. "Recalling the Wienermobile with Relish; A Frank Salute to a Slice of History: The Wienermobile." *Chicago Tribune*, February 5, 1985, D1.

——. "Unwrapping the Seasoned Pros of Hotdogdom." *Chicago Tribune*, July 29, 1976, D1.

Mayer, Oscar G., Jr. *Oscar Mayer & Co. : From Corner Store to National Processor*. New York: Newcomen Society in North America, 1970.

Oliver, Myrna. "Geogre Molchan, 82; Toured the Nation as 'Little Oscar.'" *Los Angeles Times*, May 2, 2005, Obituaries.

Peltner, Arndt. "Wealth with Wurst." *Atlantic Times*, January 2007, 20.

Rivenburg, Roy. "Return of the Wackymobile." *Los Angeles Times*, January 15, 2001.

Sherlock, Barbara. "George A. Molchan—Little Oscar for Hot-Dog Maker." *Chicago Tribune*, April 14, 2005, Obituaries.

Worthington, Rogers. "'Munchkin' Inches toward the Height of Show Biz Success." *Chicago Tribune*, November 27, 1978, B1.

York, Emily Bryson. "Oscar Mayer Jingle Maestro Dies." *Advertising Age*, August 6, 2007, 11.

Notes

Quotes from any sections on Oscar Mayer history that are not cited below come from personal interviews done by the author.

Chapter Two

7   "the commercial that took Oscar Mayer ..." : York.

7   It's now the longest-running ... : Peltner.

Chapter Three

12   Historically, the men in his family ... : *Chicago Daily Tribune*, March 12, 1955, p. B7.

12   That shop failed ... : Peltner.

12   ... in 1873, fourteen-year-old Mayer ... : *Chicago Daily Tribune*, March 12, 1955, p. B7.

12   ... becoming a butcher boy ... : Peltner.

12   ... the Schrolls left for Chicago ... : *Chicago Daily Tribune*, March 12, 1955, p. B7.

12   He apprenticed in the stockyards ... : "Oscar Mayer Foods Corp."

12   ... worked at Kohlhammer's meat market ... : *Chicago Daily Tribune*, March 12, 1955, p. B7.

12   Oscar wrote home ... : Peltner.

12   In 1883, the Mayer brothers ... : "Oscar Mayer Foods Corp."

12   "The early days weren't easy ..." : Mayer, p. 10.

13   Undaunted, the Mayer brothers borrowed ... : "Oscar Mayer Foods Corp."

13   "The Bavarian Mayer brothers ..." : "Wurst for Wares."

13   "... well-guarded little black book" : Mayer, p. 11.

13   ... customers were often waiting ... : Peltner.

13   ... packed theirs into wicker baskets ... : Mayer, p. 10.

Notes

13   ... used horse-drawn wagons ... : "The Wiener Men," p. 16.

13   "there were 43 employees ..." : Mayer, p. 10.

13   In 1911, company assets ... : "Oscar Mayer Foods Corp."

Chapter Nine

40   The company sponsored polka bands ... : "Oscar Mayer."

40   "As the fame of their product grew ..." : "The Wiener Men."

40   The company started using the name ... : "Oscar Mayer Foods Corp."

40   "one of the first companies ..." : Peltner.

41   In 1915, the company spent $2,000 ... : "Oscar Mayer Foods Corp."

41   In 1917, Oscar Mayer became the first ... : "Oscar Mayer."

41   Oscar Mayer dropped the Edelweiss name ... : Kraig, p. 64.

41   The company continued its expansion ... : "Oscar Mayer Foods Corp."

41   Perhaps the most revolutionary ... : Mayer, p. 19.

41   The yellow band appeared ... : Kraig, p. 64

41   "The Yellow Band Label ..." : Kraig, pp. 65–66.

41   "unheard of for meat products ..." : Mayer, p. 19.

Chapter Thirteen

61   "Had Carl G. Mayer put his concept ..." : Armano.

62   In the 1920s, the company used "wiener wagons" ... : Kannapell

62   In 1898, Montgomery Ward built ... : Hinckley and Robinson, p. 224.

62   "It was followed by cars ..." : Rivenburg.

62   Before landing on a mobile hot dog ... : Leroux, "Recalling the Wienermobile with relish," p. D1.

62   It was built on a Dodge chassis ... : Hinckley and Robinson, p. 224.

62   "The wiener of the original Wienermobile ..." : Leroux, "Recalling the Wienermobile with Relish," p. D1.

63   "Sales soared in the Chicago area ..." : Hinckley and Robinson, p. 224.

Chapter Eighteen

85   "We felt we had to have something ...": Deleon.

85   "You don't belong here ...": Sherlock.

86   "Raabe rode out in the open...": Leroux, "Recalling the Wiener-mobile with Relish," D1.

86   ... became a mentor ...: Oliver.

86   Molchan not only got the job ...: Sherlock.

87   "I don't know how many times ...": Leroux, "Unwrapping the Seasoned Pros of Hotdogdom," D1.

87   "It was always a madhouse...": Chicago Tonight.

87   "You can't outfox the children ...": Leroux, "Unwrapping the Seasoned Pros of Hotdogdom," D1.

87   When Molchan retired in 1987 ...: Sherlock.

87   When Molchan died in 2005 ...: Oliver.

87   Maren started out as a wrestler ...: Worthington.

87   "I used to get sick ...": Worthington.

88   "I never hit a kid yet ...": Worthington.

Chapter Twenty-two

105   After the war ...: Kraig, p. 68.

105   These Wienermobiles were designed ...: Hinckley and Robinson, p. 224.

105   They were sent to cities ...: Deleon.

106   "the old ones used to break down...": Chicago Tonight.

106   "I haven't any plans for that ...": "Meat Packer Oscar F. Mayer Is Dead at 95."

106   His son, Oscar G. Mayer ...: "Oscar Mayer Foods Corp."

106   Brooks Stevens was an innovative ...: "Brooks Stevens."

106   "There's nothing more aerodynamic ...": "Industrial Strength Design."

107   Building with fiberglass ...: "The Jeep Wienermobile."

Notes

About the Author

Dave Ihlenfeld is a television writer who has written episodes of *Family Guy* and *Malcolm in the Middle*. A graduate of the University of Missouri-Columbia, he grew up eating hot dogs in suburban Chicago. Follow him at: twitter.com/daveihl.